THE
OLD GAYS
GUIDE TO THE
GOOD LIFE

THE
OLD GAYS
GUIDE TO THE
GOOD LIFE

Lessons Learned About Love and Death, Sex and Sin, and Saving the Best for Last

By the Old Gays
of TikTok

WILLIAM
COLLINS

William Collins
An imprint of HarperCollins*Publishers*
1 London Bridge Street
London SE1 9GF

WilliamCollinsBooks.com

HarperCollins*Publishers*
Macken House, 39/40 Mayor Street Upper
Dublin 1, D01 C9W8, Ireland

First published in Great Britain in 2023 by William Collins
First published in the United States by HarperWave,
an imprint of HarperCollins*Publishers* in 2023

1

A catalogue record for this book is
available from the British Library

ISBN 978-0-00-863726-2 (hardback)
ISBN 978-0-00-863727-9 (trade paperback)

Insert art credits: All photographs courtesy of the authors.

Designed by Bonni Leon-Berman

Set in Miller Text
Printed and bound in the UK using 100%
renewable electricity at CPI Group (UK) Ltd

MIX
Paper | Supporting
responsible forestry
FSC™ C007454

This book is produced from independently certified FSC™ paper
to ensure responsible forest management.

For more information visit: www.harpercollins.co.uk/green

To our queer family who have passed before us and
to those, young and old, who have yet to find their way

Contents

Preface

OR, HOW THE OLD GAYS BECAME THE OLD GAYS

I t all started with a DM being confused for a BM.

One night five years ago, a small group of intergenerational gay men sat around a dining room table in a house in Cathedral City, California, drinking, playing board games, and getting stoned. The younger gays, John and Ryan, asked an older gay, Robert, if he knew the meanings of Gen Z and millennial catchphrases like "twerk," "gayce," and "okurrr." When Robert innocently answered that "sliding into DMs" must be about a bowel movement, John and Ryan knew they'd hit comedy gold. On a whim, they started putting Robert and his friends Mick and Bill on camera teaching them Gen Z slang. The endearing and hilarious videos went viral, and here we are. The Old Gays were born.

Today, us Old Gays—Michael "Mick" Peterson, Bill Lyons, Robert Reeves, and Jessay Martin—have more than eight million followers and have modeled for Rihanna's Savage X Fenty clothing brand. We made the *Forbes* 2022 Top Creators list. Our celeb following includes Drew Barrymore, Kristen Bell, and Lance Bass, and we have endorsement deals with major corporations Netflix, T-Mobile, and

Walgreens, not to mention adoring fans sliding into our DMs on the regular asking for our gay hands in marriage or for us to be their honorary grandpas.

Our daily TikTok posts, filmed at Robert's groovy "collab house," a stone's throw east of Palm Springs, have racked up billions of views to date. Whether we're jumping on the latest trend, like dancing to Lizzo's bop "About Damn Time," trying on dresses with a young transgender girl, or just prancing down the middle of the street in broad daylight in colorful banana hammocks and matching long gloves, we live to entertain. Our goal is to spread beauty and kindness, and make our audience's smiles shine brighter than the desert sun.

In the Old Gays' TikTok videos, we are known for baring it all, from our hairy and smooth chests to our big and not-so-big bulges in itsy-bitsy teeny-weeny bikini bottoms. Now we're ready to bare our *souls*. We want to tell the amazing unfiltered stories of our lives behind those photos. Exclusive and emotional things we've never been able to reveal in our TikTok format's short visual bursts. We are going to dive deep into our backstories, to before we even met.

We all had very different upbringings. Jessay grew up immersed in church life in the South. Robert ditched conservative Arkansas for liberal San Francisco. Bill lived a very privileged life in the fashion and design world. And Mick left the Midwest to hang with the gay bodybuilding crowd in Southern California. The one thing we have in common is that we are all very type A, which makes for "fire flames" chemistry. BTW, Mick and Robert have hooked up, but more on that later!

Obviously, the Old Gays are very . . . old and gay. So we have lots to say about the evolution of the LGBTQ+ movement through our own experiences. We were living history without even knowing it. We all grew up in the closet, had countless wild times during the gay sexual revolution, tragically lost most of our friends during the AIDS crisis (Mick and Robert are HIV+), and lived to see the unbelievable day that gay marriage became legal.

The Old Gays have about 240 years of life experience among us, but we have zero intention of slowing down. If anything, we are peaking right now. We are in the middle of a crazy second act that none of us ever saw coming. That's a huge theme of *The Old Gays Guide to the Good Life*: "Never say die!" for lack of a better phrase. You never know what's coming around the bend, so don't give up. It ain't over 'til the fat lady sings, until Mick collapses and has to be rushed to the hospital (the shocking story is in the prologue!). Robert, who found out he was HIV+ in 1987, never imagined he would make it to his seventies. He fully believed he was going to be dead within a year or two of his diagnosis.

We have been through it all (divorce, depression, bankruptcy, near-death experiences)—and we know a thing or two about a lot of different things (style, fitness, throwing fabulous dinner parties, orgy rooms). We each have a half a century's worth of personal history, from Hula-Hoops to hot hookups, through protests and parties, witnessing the chaos of the '60s to the current culture wars. We think our life experiences are universally relatable, whether you like to relax at the end of the day with a can of White Claw or a bottle of Ensure.

Honestly, one of the biggest reasons we think we are so popular is the beautiful symbiosis among generations. Younger people are genuinely curious about what the world was like when we were growing up, and there's mad respect for all we went through. The Old Gays are often stopped by young gay fans who thank them for showing what their own golden years could look like. We're having an absolute blast keeping up with "the kids." It's reenergized every single one of us. Since becoming famous on TikTok, it's like we've all been reborn.

Apparently, "grandfluencers" are very "in" at the moment, and we are "aight" with that!

We hope our story is an inspiration and our second act an aspiration. A reminder that age is just a number. That gender and sexuality are fluid. That your body is still beautiful after eight glorious but grueling decades on this planet, and you should show it off in thirst traps whenever and wherever possible. We are so lucky to have the last chapter of our lives be the best chapter of our lives. If you have any say-so, for God's sake, have the best be the last.

—Robert, Mick, Jessay, and Bill

PART I

Hi, Gays!

Prologue

GLOWING UP

The Old Gays
Origin Story

Robert sat at his desk with his head in his hands, pondering the state of his existence. To an outsider, his life must have seemed perfect. He'd retired from his high-profile job as a city planner in San Francisco, gotten rich in real estate, and moved down to Palm Springs to live that resort-fabulous retiree life and focus on his real passion: making art. At seventy-ish years old, his health was pretty good, especially considering he'd been living with HIV for nearly two decades. He had gobs of friends and enough lovers to rival Elizabeth Taylor.

But the reality was, the recession of 2008 absolutely crushed him, stripping away all his wealth and income properties, and Robert was forced to file for bankruptcy. Everything he'd worked his whole life for was being threatened or already gone. Now he was on the verge of losing his very last possession, his pride and joy: the house he was sitting in.

Back in 1990, Robert bought the house on a quaint corner in Cathedral City expecting to die in it. Nearly 80 percent of his friends had passed away from AIDS and Robert, too, had been diagnosed as HIV+. At the time, that was as good as a death sentence. Miraculously, Robert did not get sick and die. He began to create art, which he displayed in the glass-enclosed entryway like a gallery. The three-bedroom house had a giant window in the living room so you could gaze out on the beautiful pool, patio, and yard lined with lemon and grapefruit trees. A hot tub sat smack-dab in the middle of the living room. That was Robert's signature design stamp: he always put hot tubs front and center in his living rooms. He may have looked like a conservative white dude out of a Brooks Brothers catalog, but Robert always had a naughty side.

The Cat City house had its own storied history. It endured gay bashers who pelted the pool deck with eggs and threw rocks through the front windows. Hooligans also damaged one of Robert's favorite sculptures. All of this prompted Robert, who feared for his safety, to turn the keys over to rowdy vacation renters and escape to greener pastures. He fled to a dilapidated farmhouse on a five-acre ranch in Sky Valley, an unincorporated community east of Palm Springs on the other side of the 10 freeway, and cosplayed a gentleman farmer for a short stint. But the Cat City house was his real home, his heart, so when everything fell apart financially, he left Sky Valley and returned there. There was something special about the Cat City house, something about it that brought life. It always reinvigorated Robert. It was special.

Fast-forward twenty years, and Robert could no longer afford the mortgage or taxes on his dream home. He was so depressed, he'd kind of let the house—and himself—go a little. The yard was a mess. He didn't have teeth or dentures. As he sat at his desk, it crossed his mind that he should probably kill himself. At that very moment, he heard a sound behind him and turned around. A bird was standing on the floor in the doorway to his room, chirping away.

"Well, who are you?" he asked his feathered friend. The bird, a sparrow, hopped up onto the bed. Robert reached his hand out and the sparrow walked up his arm, and the two talked and chirped for a few minutes.

"Are you lost?" The bird flew out the doorway and back into the yard. Bemused, Robert put his suicidal thoughts on the back burner.

The very next day, Robert was contacted by two guys/gays who had seen his art in a Laguna Beach gallery. They'd just bought a house in the desert and asked if they could swing by and check out some of Robert's other work. "Yes," Robert said, "please do!" The next day the men bought $16,000 worth of art, enough to save Robert's house—and his life. "I believe that bird was my guardian angel."

The next mystical creature who unexpectedly entered Robert's life (and other body parts, but we'll get to that, darlings, have patience) was certainly no angel. After Robert saved his house by the skin of his (nonexistent) teeth, he knew he needed roommates to help pay the bills. So he created his own living space in the garage, which he called his casita, and placed an ad on Craigslist to rent out the three bedrooms: *Roommate/Hippie wanted: Must be nudist, LGBTQ+ and 420 lifestyle friendly.*

The first person to answer the ad was Michael "Mick" Peterson, a devilishly handsome bodybuilder with a brain for biz and a bod for sin (go ahead and say it like Melanie Griffith in *Working Girl*). Mick was not freaked out by the content of the Craigslist ad at all. "I knew what I was getting into—excuse the expression." When he walked up to the house, Robert was working in the front yard shirtless, and when he turned around, Mick thought, *Why not?*

Folks, you're hearing it here first. Robert and Mick did the deed. "It was a very in-depth interview," Robert deadpans. "He passed." After Mick moved in, there wasn't any uncomfortableness or awkwardness. It was one and done. "Most of the lasting gay friendships I have began with a sexual encounter," Mick also deadpans. "I guess it's required." (Disclaimer by Jessay: "Not all gays!")

Mick took the master bedroom with private bath. Robert had installed a wall-to-wall closet with floor-to-ceiling mirrored doors. He had dubbed it "the orgy room."

"What those mirrors could tell me," a nostalgic Mick sighs. "I decided that the 'dirty job' was up to me. I stepped up to the plate, volunteered my services, and did my best to live up to the reputation of the house. I take community service seriously. Unless the guy is a real pro at what they do, bye bye!"

It's NSA for Mick! He became the constant tenant at the Cat City house. The other two bedrooms were let to a proverbial revolving door of people with "quirks," from being broke and unable to pay rent to having sexy lingerie fetishes. The only other person besides Mick who was a fixture at Robert's house didn't live there. And that was his old friend Bill Lyons.

Bill and Robert met back in the '80s in San Francisco and had remained friends. Bill was the general manager of a large interior design showroom in SOMA, the neighborhood where Robert had been city planning the now-iconic San Francisco Giants baseball park. Robert had canvassed the area, talking to business owners and homeowners about the proposed stadium and traffic concerns. "I was impressed with the way he carried himself and addressed us," Bill recalls. "He walked so upright."

When Robert left for Palm Springs, Bill was living with his partner on a houseboat in Sausalito. In 1996, after sixteen years together, the partner left him, out of the blue, and Bill had to borrow money from his parents to keep the houseboat. After being unceremoniously dumped, Bill drank very heavily, and his mental health cratered. He was diagnosed with bipolar disorder and did outpatient therapy at Langley Porter Psychiatric Hospital at UCSF for nearly two years. Following his breakup, he also chose to be abstinent for ten years because he couldn't trust men. "It was the lowest point of my life."

By 2003, Bill was tired of living under a marine layer in San Francisco and, like Robert, had lost most of his friends to HIV. He needed a change. Like Mick, Bill moved to Palm Springs to start over. Bill had fond memories of clear blue skies and warm nights in Palm Springs, so he headed for the desert and reconnected with Robert. At first Bill was flush with cash. But the recession of 2008 crushed him.

He lost his house. Robert and Bill had breakfast together often, and Robert, through his connections, was able to get Bill the last rent-controlled apartment down the street from him in a HUD-owned building. "I would have been homeless," Bill says. Robert also offered Bill a job cleaning the Cat City house. "I was looking for anything I could do. I cleaned the bathroom and the kitchen."

Bill kept floating through life, phoning it in, as the kids might say. In Cat City, he kept busy volunteering at a food bank and writing handwritten notes for a senior center. He took yoga classes twice a week. He filled up his schedule, but his life had little direction. One bright spot was going over to see Robert, who was known for throwing legendary off-the-hook parties. "My houses had always been the party house," he says. "We had lots of crazy parties in San Francisco." He happened to live next door to Donnie Tinsley, a member of a girl gang drag group called the Balloon Girls, best known for mud wrestling and wet-Jockey-shorts contests.

The Cat City parties certainly lived up to Robert's infamous reputation. "They were so wild because with a swimming pool and an indoor spa there was ample reason for everyone to be naked. And when a whole bunch of guys get together and get naked, things happen," Robert explains. "Since I had so many bedrooms, I was able to have the master bedroom designated as the orgy room. It was well used. Lots of fun was had."

Bill, celibate at the time, wasn't partaking in *that* kind of fun. "If people were flirting with me, I didn't know it," he says. He much more enjoyed Robert's boozy dinner parties, where he could smoke pot and have intelligent conversations with Mick about any topic under the sun. "I have never met anyone smarter," Bill says. "You can ask a question on absolutely any topic, and he has a logical and correct answer."

Mick and Bill were both foodies and shared a love of cooking. Bill was impressed that Mick knew how to spatchcock a whole chicken, but they did often differ about how recipes should be prepared. They'd cheerfully banter until Mick inevitably drank too much red wine, slid down his chair onto the floor, and passed out. "We considered it a good dinner party when Mick didn't faint," Robert jokes.

"Actually," Mick intercedes, "it was a combination of wine *and weed* that led me to slither off my chair and onto the floor. Since my childhood there have been numerous times I've fainted. Doctors call this condition 'syncope.'"

There was a constant stream of people passing through Robert's fabulous house. "Actually, it was a circus," Robert says. His shenanigans didn't seem to bother his neighbors. One handsome gay neighbor, Jessay Martin, had no idea what bacchanal debauchery was going down across the street. He was oblivious to it. He did notice Robert's lovely art displayed in the window and gave a friendly wave hello here and there.

Jessay, a gospel singer who worked in a florist shop, arrived in the desert in 2013, after dealing with his own struggles, and moved across the street from Robert a year later. Jessay had survived a near-death brush with MRSA and was still grieving the end of two back-to-back ten-year relationships. One partner had died; the other had gone to prison. Jessay was devoutly Christian, a Seventh-day Adventist. He knew nothing about the orgies going on inside the house; he was happy to be a casual observer to the activity outside the house. "That was how I connected to Robert in the very beginning. He was the guy on the corner with the art in the window and saws going at odd hours when he was making his art. I looked forward to hearing him making noise out there. And if I didn't, it would concern me; I'd know something was wrong. When it's not going, you call."

Jessay was right to be concerned when the house grew uncharacteristically quiet. Robert had tired of the circus atmosphere and was becoming reclusive. Mick had begun having serious health issues. He could no longer drive because he was having extreme neurological pain and spasms in his calves, feet, hands, and fingers. He had been diagnosed with chronic CIDP, similar to MS. CIDP is rare in general but common among men with family histories of other autoimmune conditions like lupus, rheumatoid arthritis, and type 1 diabetes.

Around that time, a young guy in his thirties named John Bates moved into one of the rooms in Robert's house. John infused new energy into his housemates. He urged Robert to clean up his yard and go to the dentist, stat. He gently nudged Bill to get back into the dating game, to no avail. He tried to give all the guys new purpose in life and liven up the place.

John moved in in November 2016, the start of the holiday season. He got to know the cast of characters very well during daylong parties for Thanksgiving, Christmas, and New Year's Eve. They'd cook, drink eggnog, smoke weed, and watch sports (well, Mick would put on a football game but might be the only one who cared). They had hours-long conversations about everything under the sun. Every once in a while, John would pull Robert out for a night on the town. "John tried to reeducate me on how to go to a bar." Robert laughs.

Three months after moving in, John went to a gay bar down the street called Barracks and met Ryan Yezak, a fledgling video producer who worked at Logo TV, the first LGBTQ+ cable channel. They got serious quickly. At first, Ryan found it odd that his boyfriend lived with a bunch of "old farts," as John affectionately dubbed them. "The first time we hooked up at the house, I was like, *Where am I?*" Ryan recalls. "It felt like Willy Wonka's chocolate factory. It was a different world." The next morning John took Ryan to meet Robert in his garage studio in the back. Robert was naked and didn't have teeth. "It caught me off guard."

Mick, too, wore his birthday suit when Ryan first met him. "I tried to be open-minded, but it took several steps to understand the dynamic of this house. I questioned it at first. I had to get out of my comfort zone." But Ryan was falling in love with John and the "Old Farts" came with that package. Ryan attended their dinner parties, getting to know each member of this extended chosen family intimately. "It was more like a hippie compound, like where you can just be yourself and wear what you want—or nothing at all," Ryan explains. "'Everything goes' was the vibe."

After dinner one night, John, Ryan, and Robert were getting stoned when one of them used some kind of Gen Z catchphrase, which prompted Robert to be like, *Huh?* John suggested that Ryan put the older guys on camera for shits and giggles. As soon as he pressed record, he got chills that were multiplying. The comedy—and the chemistry—was immediate. "It was so organic," Ryan says. "You couldn't put this together if you tried."

John officially changed the name "Old Farts" into the less stinky-sounding "Old Gays." Magic from moment one. They did a longer YouTube video in which the guys tried to decipher "new slang" from the younger gay generation. Their answers were adorable, of courz.

Bop: "A bebop was a good tune," Bill said.

Beat for the Gods: "One wild masturbation session," Mick replied.

Okurr: "Okay, you're real rad," Robert said. "This is the kind of thing the Kardashians would sit around and do all afternoon."

Even though the Old Gays were immediately a hit and always met with a positive response with every video posted, there were two concerning problems going on behind the scenes. The first was that it was obvious that this newfangled vaudevillian act was too white. "We needed to open up that club a little bit more to be more diverse and inclusive," Ryan says.

There would be no casting call. One day while Robert was watering his plants, his neighbor Jessay pulled up to the nearby stop sign, rolled down his window, and began talking to Robert about seeing the Old Gays on YouTube. Robert's exact words were, "We're looking for some diversity." Jessay said, "Oh, you need some color?" They both laughed, and Jessay handed Robert one of his business cards.

He didn't need much persuasion. He was in. The rest is history.

"It was so sweet the way it happened," Jessay adds. "I felt like I was adopted by all of them."

Mick remembers being introduced to Jessay and thinking what an effervescent human being he was. But his second thought was, *"Does he know what he's getting into?* Because at that point, I didn't even know what I was getting into. I felt a little sorry for him."

By the time Jessay joined the Old Gays, Mick's health was in crisis.

He'd had a seizure, the cause of which has never been determined. After losing consciousness, he crashed his body and walker into the orgy room's mirrors. Robert found Mick unconscious with a giant bleeding gash over his eye and called 911. While he was unconscious in the ambulance, the paramedics prepped him for a ventilator. Fortunately, it would not be needed.

Mick recalls being placed in a bright, shimmering white light. "I was seeming to hover. It felt like I was suspended in a black void. I listened to a disembodied and nongendered voice say to me, 'Look, you can come with me now or . . . go back.' In reply to this voice I answered and said, 'I'll go back. There are things that I need to complete and make right.'"

Mick was kept in the trauma center/ICU for eleven days. After neurosurgery to repair damage to his left eye, he was taken to a nursing home. "When I arrived there, staff didn't think I'd survive, let alone ever walk again," Mick says. After he was discharged, he returned to the safety of the Cat City house using a walker. A full recovery, though, seemed uncertain.

"Mick almost threw in the towel," Ryan says, looking back. "He progressively got worse and was consumed by his health challenges." His fatigue and pain were so intense that on the night of May 11, 2020, he overdosed on gabapentin. The paramedics were called again. Mick was taken to the ER and later admitted to the hospital.

After another stint in assisted living, Mick moved into a motel down the hill from Robert's house to convalesce. Robert saw how hard he was fighting to get back on his feet and stay alive. Robert paid him a visit one afternoon and told him he wanted him to come back home: "Focus on getting better." On Mick's sixty-fourth birthday, he returned to the Cat City house again and hasn't left since. Mick didn't know how he'd be greeted by all the guys; he was worried that they were mad at him for derailing or disrupting the Old Gays momentum. But they welcomed him back with open arms. "I prayed for him, I really did," Jessay says.

The rest of the guys were so unsure he might not survive this set-back, they prepared for the possibility that he would be leaving this earth. They filmed a video paying homage to Mick in their own way. Mick's never seen the video, and it's never been released.

Mick was a mess when he first arrived home. He could hardly speak, could barely do anything. In fact, in TikToks from that time, he can be seen holding on to a walker. Not long after Mick's return, the Old Gays went to LA to shoot a video. One morning Mick came out of his hotel room and walked down the hallway without a shirt on. Jessay had never seen him like that, and while ogling his chiseled physique blurted out, "Mick, how do you do it?" Jessay told him he looked per-fect, and his body looked beautiful. "I do it for the people!" Mick joked.

Jessay believes performing again with the Old Gays was the turn-ing point for Mick's health. "People see you, but they don't know what's going on inside. He had gone through so much, I'd seen him at death's door, but he decided to get back to living." Mick started treating his body like a temple, the way he used to, and received infu-sions for his autoimmune disease every two weeks. His balance and strength, mentally and physically, came roaring back. "This old man came rolling home. It was total awesomeness to me," Jessay says. "Now you don't ever see him with a shirt *on*."

With Mick healthy again and Jessay on board, there was no stop-ping the new and improved Old Gays. The chemistry among them was catalytic. Mick took on the part of the bawdy and edgy senior, armed with shocking and often unexpected one-liners. Jessay, the resident paragon of grace and good behavior, could be relied upon for a hilar-ious and genuine reaction to the audacity of the others. Bill was the wild card: you never knew if he was going to charm you and make you feel brilliant or put you in your place with a verbal slap. Robert was always game; he'd show up for anything we put out there.

The Old Gays blew up on TikTok, gaining millions of followers, making appearances in mainstream media like *The Drew Barrymore Show* and the *Today* show, and going viral regularly. Some of their posts have been seen by one hundred million people. The first time they were recognized in public will go down as one of the most memorable. After dinner at a restaurant in LA, all the guys were standing on a curb waiting for an Uber. A young woman ran by with headphones on, saw the Old Gays, and shouted with glee, "Oh my God, TikTok!" She never even stopped running.

At first the Old Gays were simply delighted that their antics were entertaining so many people. It all went to the next level when they started getting messages that their videos were helping people. Just for being themselves. Maybe there was something else going on here besides good old-fashioned camp.

One message was from a nineteen-year-old boy named Itay. He wrote:

First of all just know that I'm your hugest fan. as a part of the lgbt community, seeing you walking with so much pride and showing light to the world helped me get through some really hard times. It took me a while to get to know myself and accept who I actually am.

Itay couldn't possibly know that the Old Gays were still figuring that out themselves, even after being on the planet for six or seven decades. This is kind of meta, but *being* the Old Gays changed their lives for the better, too. "We all had these incredible lives," Bill says. "And then each of us hit these rock-bottom moments and thought, *Maybe this is it for me. Like, maybe life is really over.*"

It wasn't over. Not by a long shot. What all the Old Gays have learned through this process is this: you never know what's coming around the corner, so please do not give up hope, no matter how low you get, no matter how awful whatever you're going through. Second, third, fourth—endless—acts are waiting for you, as long as you're on this earth. Life can turn on a dime. Trust the universe to turn it all around. What really matters is community. The OGs found each other, became a community of friends late in life, and helped each other through tough times. By luck and some inspired ideas—and some daring skimpy outfits!—they expanded that community to include millions. That's a bit of a unicorn last act, admittedly, but it's never too late to find community. That's where the magic happens. And it can happen right where you are now.

Bill wasn't sure he'd ever have sex again after his breakup. "I started reading comments that people thought I was hot." He laughs. "Old Gays not only gave me purpose, it made me realize that people want me. I got a proposal for marriage, from a guy in Turkey who said his life would not be complete until he talked to me on the phone." Needless to say, Bill is dating again.

Jessay was the most social of the group but also the most closed off when it came to sharing the gay side of his life publicly. "When we first started, he would often say, 'I don't share that' or 'I don't do that,'" Ryan says. "The greatest turnaround for Jessay has been seeing him open up and be himself at this age."

"I owe my new life to Robert. He's been a wonderful friend, beyond the call of duty," says Mick. Back to beefcake form, he explains, "I am a bionic man and a medical miracle," he stresses. "I've had two cataract surgeries, one hip replaced, am HIV undetectable and kept alive thanks to a five-hour infusion of immunoglobulin every other week. The lesson of going through immense pain and suffering has taught me compassion for any human being less fortunate than me. By fate or divine intent, I am thankful to be alive. For this second chance. When things get tough on set, when my pain and fatigue seem too much to bear, I tell myself to focus on the task at hand. To make my queer family laugh. To forget for just one TikTok minute their troubles."

John and Ryan got married and moved four houses down the street.

And Robert? Well, the Cat City home he nearly lost in bankruptcy is now the epicenter of one of the most beloved TikTok acts of all time. It may be as recognizable to this online generation as the *Brady Bunch* house was to older generations. "Without this house, there's really no us," Robert says.

Oh, and BTW, there's still a room available to rent. Clothing optional, of course.

1

THE GLUE: ROBERT

"Bob is just one of the smartest people I ever met,
but you wouldn't know it just looking at him."

—JESSAY

The world has always revolved around Robert, Bob to his close friends. We don't mean that in an icky, self-centered way. Quite the opposite. Robert, seventy-nine years young as of this writing, has always carried himself with an air of quiet confidence and go-with-the-flow attitude. His easy, breezy, beautiful CoverGirl vibe doesn't come from being a lifelong marijuana smoker. Well, not entirely. From his childhood in Arkansas up until now, people have always gravitated toward Robert and orbited around the universe he creates. He builds community around him, literally when he was a city planner, but also with his friends. He's always the ringleader wherever he goes—from his wild days in San Francisco in the '70s and '80s to hosting nudist dinner parties in his house in Palm Springs. Robert, an analytical city planner by day (he helped create the SF Giants stadium—mmm, that crab sandwich), is also a well-known artist and sculptor. People in his neighborhood in Cat City regularly drive by his house to see what piece he's displaying in the front window. As we said earlier, a few homophobes have even thrown rocks through those windows. They probably just have a crush on Bob. Who wouldn't? He's a tall drink of water and adds comedy and levity to any conversation/situation, whether intentional or not.

Nudist Etiquette 101

I've always preferred to be in my birthday suit. At a very young age, when I was back in Arkansas, we lived at the edge of town, so my brothers and I would only need to walk a few properties over from our house and be in the middle of nowhere. There was a huge horse pasture and a creek and a hillside that would bloom with clover in the spring. I can remember taking hikes by myself over there, finding the most secluded spots, taking off my clothes, and running through the woods and feeling so free. I'd climb trees naked and pretend I was Tarzan. It was my escape from society's pressures about how I was supposed to be. When I went to St. Louis for college, that's the first time I discovered bathhouses. By the time I got to San Francisco, I started hosting my own nudist parties/orgies.

When people don't have clothes on, pretty much anything goes. When you're in a room full of men and everyone's naked, there's not much casual conversation. You're mostly just going for the pile, but there is etiquette and standards of being respectful. Here are some dos and don'ts for hosting and attending nudist gatherings:

For the Host
- Create a mood. Make a hard-driving playlist and put porn on the TVs. Candles can be dangerous for bare bottoms and dangling body parts; opt instead for mirrors and rosy-red lighting, which makes the skin glow.
- Don't allow junk on your good furniture. It's okay to make clear in the form of a friendly note that certain spots in your home are not suitable for ass cheeks and other body parts and fluids.
- Speaking of fluids, make sure everyone hydrates! Provide refreshments for breaks in the action. People will be parched. Oh, and don't forget the bowl of condoms; even if nobody uses them, it's good form to provide them gratis.

For Guests
- Bring a little Dopp bag. You'll need lube, a towel, and party favors for your new friends. Perhaps some poppers.
- You can look *and* touch. You don't have to look people in the eyes or pretend not to stare. You're allowed to oogle all the beautiful bodies and make sexy comments. It's all out there for everybody to see, so it's not like anyone's hiding anything.
- However, don't intrude unless you've been invited. This is the most important rule. If you find someone attractive and you

want to get to know them better, and you're trying to get their attention and they're obviously not interested, don't push it. There should be an accepted understanding that some people are attracted and some aren't. If there are two or three people who seem to be really enjoying themselves, let them have their fun and just observe.

How to Host Epic Dinner Parties

- Invite a foodie who knows how to cook.
- Limit the guest list to six people. That's best for good conversation and camaraderie. If you invite more, you'll be cleaning up for two days.
- Invite a new, interesting, even mysterious person who your group doesn't know. It's great to get their perspective on life, plus it's not unheard-of that they will end up getting to know someone at the party much better by the end of the night—hint, hint, wink.
- Don't invite frenemies, unless you want *Real Housewives*–style table flipping and drama.
- Put one unique item on your menu. For example, I really got into fixing artichokes in different ways for a hot minute.
- Smoke lots of pot before you eat. Everyone will rave about your cooking, even if you screw it all up.
- Let the wine and gossip flow freely and endlessly.
- Put on a pop hits playlist and dance all over the house.
- Push someone in the pool (if you have one) with all their clothes on. Just make sure they aren't carrying their cell phone first!

2

THE BON VIVANT: BILL

"Bill will do anything, really anything, for you."

—MICK

B ill has described the Old Gays as the most exciting thing that has ever happened to him in his seventy-nine years—and that's saying a lot because the man has lived quite a life. "I haven't been rich, but I've been very privileged." Bill has had a fabulous, chic life working in the modeling, fashion, and interior design industries in LA and San Francisco as a handsome young gay man in the '70s and '80s. At first glance, Bill seems like Charlotte from *Sex and the City* because he gives off a super-conservative, innocent vibe, but he also has always had a little devil on his shoulder nudging him to live a little. Back in the day, Bill hung out with the highfliers in Beverly Hills and, in his decorating years, partied with Steve Wynn and Liberace and served tea at lunch with Phyllis Diller and Johnny Carson at the famed Beverly Hills Hotel. Today, Bill loves dressing up in drag or down to his skivvies. He also loves when people slide into his DMs.

From Drab to Fab: My Best Fashion and Lifestyle Tips

I've always had a taste for the finer things in life. I hate to admit it because it sounds kind of snobby, but I'm into opera (*Tosca* is my fave), art, and fine food. My parents' high school graduation present to me was sending me to have dinner with the PR rep for Perino's, one of the most legendary celebrity hangouts during Hollywood's Golden Age. Sinatra was known to tickle the ivories there, while Joan Crawford and Bugsy Siegel noshed on the legendary pressed duck. I've also been to the French Laundry twice. I have a collection of old *Architectural Digest* magazines dating back to the first issue in 1923. I have a talent for walking into a store and picking out the most expensive thing. I worked in upscale men's clothing stores in my teens and twenties and have been into fashion and design ever since. Here's how to look your best every day:

Start with a K.I.S.S.: That means Keep It Simple, Sir!

Don't copy anyone: Everyone should have their own style; don't just repeat what you see on other people.

Dress for success: The Casual Friday look is out of control. Everyone looks like slobs nowadays. Put effort into what you wear out in the world.

But don't spend a lot of money: I was poor for so long, I can't stomach paying $200 for a bathing suit. I go to Macy's now and find incredible deals.

Buy one good suit: No one wears suits anymore these days, but if you're called to an occasion suddenly, or, God forbid, a memorial service, it's very important to show respect to the people you are honoring. A good suit and tie is a basic for every wardrobe. Twenty years ago you could get a Brioni custom suit for $2,500. Now they're like $10,000. There's really no reason anyone needs custom. You can easily put together a great look for under $150. Navy or gray suits are appropriate for just about any occasion.

... And a Speedo! I just love Speedos.

Skip the latest trend: In the '70s, bell-bottoms were so in, but all that extra fabric bouncing around reminded me of a clown. I was never a fan of neon in the '80s or baggy clothes in the '90s. Tight pants are always in fashion, though.

Brighten up your look: Brown and black can get so drab. Ask a salesperson in a store to tell you honestly what fun colors look good on you. For example, I'm too pale to wear yellow or orange; it washes me out. I wear a lot of blue because it matches my eyes.

Step out of your comfort zone: Since the Old Gays, I'm much more experimental. I actually wear lime green now! And one-piece women's bathing suits, but that's another story.

Moisturize your skin: Companies come to us and they send us their complete line of grooming accessories. One included a face wash and little things that you could put on your eyes. Some of 'em were cucumbers, some of 'em were gold. And then they sent us a whole series of masks that we could put on again for exfoliating.

Groom: Beards are all the rage, but sometimes they just look horrible, like Yosemite Sam. Hairy can be scary if you don't trim and maintain.

Shave your balls: I had my first experience when the Old Gays re-created the shower scene from Lil Nas X's video. Basically, it was shot nude. So I went to a salon here in town and had it done so it looked neat. But Manscaped is a great tool, because if you go to a salon to get your chest shaved or your bush trimmed, it's easily $90. Manscaped also has special ointments for your scrotum for a very, very clean cut. Honestly, it's just more attractive to shave your balls, plus it helps accentuate your size down there.

Don't overaccessorize: Belts, jewelry, pocket squares, all are individual choices. Just remember what Coco Chanel famously advised, and I'm paraphrasing here: "To become the best-dressed person you can, take off the last thing you put on before you go out."

I Remember When . . . I Wore the Trendiest Outfits

BILL: I wore white buck suede shoes with pink soles and used a bunny bag. A bunny bag contained a white powder to keep your bucks clean if they got dirty. In school it also denoted status. I was a cheerleader. I was in class council. I was on the debate team. I was a "white buck." That had an entirely new meaning in West Covina. It meant I had lots of friends, got good grades, and was going to college.

MICK: In the fall of '68, during my first year of junior high, my grandmother bought me an outfit from the wild 1960s Carnaby Street in London—bell-bottoms and a very colorful shirt with piping. Very Mick Jagger! I thought I looked "cool." Then a freshman swaggered up to me, called out "Fag," and tried to punch me out.

BILL: In the '70s I wore bell-bottoms and Nehru suits. And Nik-Nik polyester shirts with crazy designs that fit real snug, to a T. The collar opened all the way down to your belly button and the look was made complete by wearing about fourteen gold chains. Basically the *Saturday Night Live* "wild and crazy guys" look but without irony. This was the lounge lizard era—it was all about men showing off their masculinity by wearing extremely tight pants that left little to the imagination and exposing lots of chest hair. It was all very gay, but straight men did it, too. Gay men have always been at the forefront of fashion.

JESSAY: There was one year I wore green only. I asked my mom later, "How did you do that?" We were not rich, but she did it. I loved it. The bigger the collar, the happier I was. Girl, so much polyester, I'm surprised I didn't burst into flames. The higher the heel, the closer to God. I love platform heels. They changed me. I couldn't help myself. I had one person call me a sissy. I said, "So?"

ROBERT: I was never very fashion-conscious. I was in Brooks Brothers suits. At the time it worked.

BILL: I once bought myself a white, heavy, twill, double-breasted suit and upstaged my boss at a party. He was so pissed.

3

THE PEACEFUL ONE: JESSAY

"I see him as someone who is literally coming out now. He's embracing his gayness. I'm not gonna say 'sexuality' 'cause I think he's always been a sexual person. But he's really enjoying who he is right now."

—ROBERT

essay doesn't identify with any of the *Sex and the City* or *Golden Girls* characters because none were women of color. "I grew up being myself from birth," he says. Jessay, sixty-nine, has never taken life seriously. He cries a lot but only because he's so happy. "It's all love. It's all positivity. That's how I was raised." Jessay is a professional singer, and most of his life has revolved around music and religion. He grew up in Greeneville, Tennessee, and his parents shielded him from racism and homophobia by insulating him in the church world. Later, when constantly touring as a professional singer, Jessay lived in a bubble. Jessay started out being the least comfortable with performing TikToks and sharing intimate details about his life. At first, when asked to do things like dress in drag, his response was, "Nope, nope, nope." He was body-shaming himself. Now he choreographs the Old Gays' signature dance moves and is front and center and always up for getting down. He still doesn't understand why the world is interested in four old men, but he's learned to accept and say, "So it is!"

My Favorite Church Music

I don't even like secular music; I'm all about gospel. We all have our ways of pulling ourselves out of the dungeon, and that's music for me. Here are my top five heavenly tunes:

1. "Great Is Thy Faithfulness." This is my number one song to sing and to hear. It's a wonderful hymn. I first sang it at my mom's funeral and also the funeral of my partner, Don. It's a simple melody but so powerful. "Great is thy faithfulness, oh God, my father, there is no shadow of turning with thee. Thou changest not thy compassions, they fail not; as thou hast been,

thou forever wilt be. Great is thy faithfulness! Great is thy faithfulness! Morning by morning, new mercies I see." That's my favorite part. "All that I have needed thy hand hath provided. Great is thy faithfulness, Lord unto me!" I have an accompanist that makes me sing it like never before each time. I Jessay-ize it. It's a song of encouragement. When I'm really down, I will go stand in front of a mirror and sing that from the depths of my soul because there's good reverb in a bathroom. It can lift me out of the valley so quickly. It makes me feel alive again.

2. "Jesus, You're the Center of My Joy" by the late Walter Hawkins. And, chiiiild, I just get ugly.

3. "I Can Only Imagine" by Tamela Mann. This song fills me with the excitement of meeting Jesus for the first time. How will I act and feel? That is what the song is about. I'm retiring from my job as a full-time staff singer at my church this year, and this is the song I chose to be my last solo offering. It's perfection. I'm going out with a bang. It's going to be a hard day for me. I've been singing at my church since 1986. I'm going to miss it.

4. "This Too Shall Pass" by Yolanda Adams. This is about grief and sorrow over losing a loved one. I've lost my lover, my mom, and my three sisters. And I've had to learn to move forward without having them in my life to lean on. The pain passed, and I learned to live in the present instead of wondering, *What if?*

5. "I Look to You" by the late, great Whitney Houston. I recently got this song after listening to it and hearing Whitney singing about her self-lost feelings. We only have God to look to, and maybe she was just crying out and looking for His/Her strength and love to carry her peacefully to her rest.

4

THE
WILD ONE:
MICK

"I admire his perseverance and his will to live."

—ROBERT

A once-upon-a-time nice boy from Minnesota, Mick moved to California the second after his college diploma was handed to him. Free of the soybean straitjacket that was the Midwest, our Mick was ready to swing from the rafters. He ate many a forbidden fruit. He was born with a rebellious nature and wanderlust. "I see this as a practiced desire to shock." Think Samantha from *Sex and the City* with a dash of Dorothy from *The Golden Girls* (they have the same basso voice). When Mick first arrived in Southern California, he had not yet embraced all its diversity and subcultures. By chance he met a former Mr. Olympia on the gay beach in Laguna. It was John Tristram, who then introduced Mick to the world of competitive and professional bodybuilding. "John and I shared a pursuit of the extreme and freakish." Mick laughs. "The sex was beyond fabulous, too."

How to Be a Beefcake Like Me (Even When It's Hard to Get Out of Bed)

When I was bullied in high school, my dad bought me a weight set from a Sears catalog. Working out became a lifelong passion that has never wavered. I remember in graduate school, my acting teachers at UC Irvine kept saying, "Don't work out so much, you'll become stiff, and you won't have any movement." Meanwhile I was watching bodybuilders do the splits. So what are you telling me about not being agile? Working out . . . dull and repetitive as it is, has proven to be a lifesaver for me. I rely on exercise to get me through the toughest days. Regardless of age, movement is essential to a happy, healthy life. Here are my top ten fitness tips for seniors:

1. Nutrition is more important than exercise. Consider what you are putting into your body . . . at all times.

2. Drink two large glasses of water every night before you go to bed. Since you're gonna be up to pee anyway, you might as well stay hydrated. It's good for your skin and your mood, and you will also lose fat.

3. Take supplements. I take extra sodium, potassium, and magnesium. Discuss with your doctor what you're lacking.

4. Substitute plant protein for animal protein. You don't have to go full-on vegan. Try eating lentils, black-eyed peas, and nuts instead of fish and meat. I have a weakness for a big bowl of Tuscan white bean soup.

5. No carbs—simple or complex—after sunset. While you're sleeping, your body converts sugar to fat.

6. Instead of three meals per day, try eating five or six. That will cut down your portion sizes.

7. Join a gym—the membership will be partly covered by Medicare.

8. Hire a trainer who will establish an exercise program for you. We all have medical conditions—arthritis, autoimmune diseases, heart, etc. There are experienced and highly knowledgeable trainers who know how to help you. Find out who they are. Check with your primary care physician or physical therapist. They may have a list of qualified instructors to refer you to. I've found many excellent trainers who promote themselves on social media. Invest your time in a trainer who will analyze your situation, give you a routine, and work directly with you. You know, train together!

9. Take up ballroom or square dancing. Dancing of any kind burns fat and strengthens your bones. Plus, it's fun!

10. Make resistance training and exercise a vital part of your life. From experience—give yourself six months of consistent activity and training. This will boost your metabolic rate. That's when you will see amazing results. 💪

PART II

Life Lessons Learned Along the Way

5
COMING OUT
Living That Sissy Life

I n our early days, none of us could be "out"—it wasn't an option. We didn't even think of ourselves as being in the closet; we didn't have the language yet to articulate how we felt. We just pleasured ourselves to the guys in Sears catalogs, kept our mouths shut, and molded to society. We all left our homes and families on our own with blind faith, sensing deep in our hearts there was a place for us somewhere. The nascent support systems may have been weak at the time, but our determination to find our tribe was strong. Also, we were thirsty, or as we called it back in the day, hot and bothered! Love is always one of life's greatest motivators, isn't it? Through the turbulence of war, the struggles for civil and equal rights, the sexual revolution, and the conservative backlash, we all managed to come out proudly in the '60s and '70s, way ahead of the curve. Looking back, we were living history, openly and fearlessly, but in the moment, we had no clue that living our daily lives as we wanted to (rather than trying to deny our sexuality) would help ignite the Velvet Revolution.

BABY GAYS

BILL: I grew up in Covina, California, the first of five children. My parents owned a restaurant called the Lyons Den. It was fancy; we served lobster and prime rib on Friday and Saturday nights. I worked there as far back as I can remember—I think I filed my first Social Security taxes when I was just ten years old, like Shirley Temple!

JESSAY: I grew up in Greeneville, Tennessee. I didn't know we were poor because everything I asked for, somehow, I got it. I rode go-karts and shot BB guns with the neighborhood boys. My life was really, really good. I am the only child of Benjamin and Jannie Martin. My dad was married previously, so I had three half sisters and one stepsister. My dad was a police officer—we called him the "Black Barney Fife"—and my mom was a housekeeper. We kids cleaned our own house because the last thing my mother wanted to do when she got home from work was clean up our mess. That included washing dishes. She taught us how to do it. On occasion, she would let me go to work with her. It was another world to me. My eyes were giant saucers when I saw how well white people lived. We didn't have all the fancy stuff that they had. Her employers were always so good to us kids. My sister and I always got birthday and Christmas gifts from them. I'm still connected to them. The memory of my mom brings us together. It's nice hearing her former employers talk about her.

I was extremely close to my mom. She was pure love, she exuded good, she was perfection, what I would think God is like. If she doesn't make it to heaven, there is none. She always let me hug and kiss on her. She was always there for me. She disciplined me, but she never yelled at me. Which was harder for me because I'd rather have the yelling and get it done with instead of "Mommy loves you, and it hurts me more than it does you." I said, "Please, girl."

ROBERT: I was born and raised in Jonesboro, Arkansas. I had very supportive parents and two brothers. We were lower middle-class. I give a lot of credit to my parents because I think one of the things they did instill into us was a really good work ethic, which we took with us and has been with us our entire lives. My father was a shoe salesman and repairman and had his own storefront business. My mom worked the counter, and as we kids got older, we helped out on Saturdays, because that was the big day when all the farmers came into town and did their shopping. We had racks and racks of shoes in open boxes. By third grade, I worked the cash register and waited on people. I was the one who greeted the farmers at the door and said, "Hi, can I help you?" I was a natural. I didn't mind working there because a bakery counter shared our space, so whenever I wanted a pastry it was very handy. I have a sweet tooth to this day.

MICK: I grew up in a Minnesota rough-and-tumble mining town ninety miles from Canada.

My dad was a World War II veteran and a dentist. My mother was a schoolteacher until she quit to raise my three sisters and me. When I was six months old, she was diagnosed with lupus and hospitalized for two and a half years. At that very crucial time of my life, I had no mother. My father was busy with his practice; thus, we were raised by housekeepers. We went through thirty housekeepers! That is, until a plump Finnish woman named Susan joined my family. She was kind and loving. Susan took care of my sisters and me for years after my mother was discharged from the hospital. One of my earliest memories is that of my mother when she returned. I remember the color of the suit she wore. It was blue. A beautiful brooch pinned to her suit. And how she looked at me. It was a mother's love. Perhaps experienced for the first time ever. The last memory of my mother is of that same look . . . of her motherly love for me more than forty years on.

Looking back, I believe that the emotional and psychological trauma of being separated from my mother, and the dysfunction that characterized the first three critical years of my life, have left their mark. To this day I struggle with intimacy and trust.

BORN THIS WAY

ROBERT: Various people made comments about me when I was growing up. For a number of years, we had a housekeeper who helped my mom take care of the kids and do laundry. She was very warm and friendly, and I remember her saying more than once, "That Bobby is so pretty." She implied that I was so feminine that I should have been a girl. There never ever was any criticism or downgrading of homosexuals. She was just the first person who figured out what was happening and expressed it.

JESSAY: I always saw myself less as a sissy, more as a strong Black woman. I didn't even know men could fall in love with each other. I didn't know I was gay because I'd never heard the term. I'd never even heard the word "homosexual." I just liked being around men. I figured it out as I got older. One boy did call me a queer, and it scared me, so I immediately blurted out, "So?" When I said it, my body inside went, *No, you didn't.* He did bother me one more time, but he was Caucasian, and I got all my Black friends together and they held him down while I cut off his bangs with scissors. Then I threw his pasty bangs at him. He never bothered me again. I didn't take stuff from people back then. I was kind, but I would stand up to you. I'm still that way. But now I've learned not to yell and go crazy. I let you rant, and I just shut down and sit there and stare at you.

MICK: In public school I liked being in plays as much as I liked playing football. Until I was bullied in the sixth grade, I didn't see myself as "different." I knew that I wasn't well-liked. There was something about me that was "singular." Then somebody called me a "femme," which left me feeling devastated. Not just alone. Kinda threatened. My dad had taught me that if anybody picked a fight with me, I was to walk away. After this boy bullied me, my dad bought me a weight-lifting set from the Sears Roebuck catalog. I added one entire size to my neck, which made me appear more formidable. Ha ha! The next time the guy called me a femme, I threw him into a snowbank.

BILL: I was gay, and I knew it from the age of three. It's a cliché, but baby, I was born this way. I was protective of myself from a very young age because I was aware I was different and it was not okay to tell anyone. I never played doctor with the other kids; I stayed away from anything that would take me in that direction. One time, when I was about nine, I was in the shower after swimming at a friend's house and a boy reached over to touch my dick and I pushed his hand away. I wanted to do it, but knew I absolutely should not because word might get around that I liked to play with boys' peepees.

I did everything I could to overcome it and act straight, but alas. It was impossible to change who I was. My father did everything he could, too, and was likewise unsuccessful in changing me. Like, he made me quit ballet when I was nine, as if that would stop the gay. The gay was never going away. He knew it, I knew it, everyone in my family knew it. In fact, the only time I ever saw my father hit any of his kids was when I was ten years old. We were in the kitchen one morning, and my mom, my dad, my brother, and I were arguing about something. My brother said, "Well, he's nothing but a sissy!" My dad slapped him. It was not ever going to be acceptable to have homosexuals in our family.

DADDY ISSUES

JESSAY: You could say we all have major daddy Issues! We'd prefer to have zaddy issues. If you met my dad, he was handsome and hilarious, he would have you in stitches. I guess he loved me, but he didn't like me because I wasn't the son he pictured in his head. He was possibly disappointed that I was gay. He picked on me, just constant putdowns. You're not doing this, you're not doing that. I couldn't do anything right, even mowing the yard. When he walked in the house, the whole dynamic changed. We walked on eggshells and literally had to whisper. My mom always said don't say anything bad about anybody, and not him either. She always told me, "That's your dad. You have to love him, but you don't have to like him. He's doing the best he can." I hated this man for a long time. The Old Gays did a Father's Day video, and I had nothing to say about my dad. I said, "I don't even know him." Ryan asked me to try. So I looked at his picture and thought, *Who are you? Where were you when I was growing up?* And the anger finally fell off. I asked myself, *Why are you holding on to this? He's dead.* And all of a sudden, I loved this man, and I have been happy ever since. It was healing. But we have to do things in our own time. Now I tell people my funny, silly side is my dad and my gentle, mothering side is my mom.

BILL: My father had quite a few faults. He borrowed money from everyone, including me, and never paid anyone back. He had a lot of charisma, and he was a great showman, but he had zero parenting skills. He played favorites. He idolized my brother because he was a basketball star who got a scholarship to UCLA under coach John Wooden. After my dad passed away, we found a huge scrapbook with a custom-made cover on it in raised copper dedicated to my brother's athletic career. My sister and I joked, "Where's the Bill book? Where's the Julie book?" My dad was always doing the wrong thing, which caused a lot of problems in his relationship with my mom. She was a beautiful woman. She absolutely had no judgments, and I never heard her swear in my life. She never gossiped. My mom and I had a very, very close relationship, I absolutely adored her. I think my mother always knew I was gay maybe because in high school she was kind of a tomboy and played on the baseball team. Anyway, when I was sixteen, my mother took me aside one afternoon and said, "Would you mind if I divorced your dad?" I said, "No, not at all." She didn't ask anyone else for their opinion.

GOING AGAINST THE GRAIN

ROBERT: My dad's attempt to try to make sure that we were being raised in a straight household was to take all of us boys fishing, hunting, or to the gravel pit to shoot tin cans all day. In the seventh grade I went out for the football team because my older brother played football. I remember going to the very first practice: I was out there on the field doing my thing, and I got tackled by five guys. That was enough of that! I dropped football and joined the band the next day. I played baritone saxophone.

BILL: After the female cheerleaders at my school gave a great big cheer to the opposing team when they made a touchdown, they added male cheerleaders. It was totally sexist, but it was the '50s—what can I say? There were two of us. Very few schools had male cheerleaders. I was also very into clothes. I dressed to the nines for school even though the only selection I had was the local JCPenney. I never owned a pair of Levi's. I always wore chinos or corduroy pants, and I always had good shoes. I spent a lot of money on clothes. My father asked my brother to count how many shirts I had in my closet—by the time I was a senior I had about one hundred—and he forbade me to buy any more shirts. He thought I dressed too well for high school and spent too much money on fashion. He said, "Why do you dress up every day?" I ignored him and was handsomely rewarded with the superlative of "Snappy Dresser" in my high school yearbook. So it was worth being criticized incessantly by my father.

JESSAY: I was in an all-Black school up until the sixth grade; then integration happened. They shut our school down, of course, and we spread out to different white schools. It was the loneliest time of my life, because I was the only Black person in all of my classes, except choir. All I wanted to do was sing the Negro national anthem. I'll never forget, I sat in the front row the first day, and Judy Kramer asked me why I was sitting in the front row. I snapped, "Well, why not?" She said, "You're right," and she's still one of my dearest friends to this day. Before integration, I didn't know any white people except the boys that my mom worked for. The funniest thing was my first time in PE with these white guys. We were in the shower, and I turned and took a peek and laughed. "Guys, what's wrong with your butts?" They all looked like that little white girl on the sunscreen bottle with the dog pulling her pants down. "Martin, it's a suntan!" I'd never experienced that. Of course, I got a boner and had to turn on the cold water. I was laughing even then—but then I didn't look anymore!

CELEBRITY CRUSHES

ROBERT: Keep in mind that in the environment that I was growing up in in the '50s and '60s, publicly, there were no overtly gay people in the media. It was really suppressed. But there were male singers I was very enamored with—Fabian, Bobby Darin, and Elvis. I like to dance!

JESSAY: I loved Tom Jones. My, he just moved!

BILL: Every Saturday morning my parents would give my brother and me a quarter each, and we would go to the local movie house because they started at ten a.m. They showed cartoons, then a feature film, and more cartoons after that. I had a special affinity for Buster Crabbe, who played Flash Gordon. I also had a crush on Hopalong Cassidy. And my parents took me to see *The Kid from Texas,* with Audie Murphy playing Billy the Kid. I walked out of there crying because he had gotten shot. I was just crushed. My parents thought I wasn't ready for shoot-'em-up movies. They didn't know I had fallen in love. That was my first recognition that I liked men. And I knew instinctively it shouldn't be told.

MICK: I bought all of Elton John's early albums . . . and I stress "early years." Even earlier, though, there were the "tough guys, but with a heart" stars like Clint Walker on television's *Cheyenne,* who I followed. Robert Conrad was cut, hairy, and hot! On prime-time TV he was placed in one over-the-top predicament after another. Yeah! It was bondage on full display during episodes of *The Wild Wild West.* Bare, hairy-chested, and defined Mr. Conrad was in full glory . . . restrained and flexing. Last there was Mike Henry, linebacker at USC, and for the Pittsburgh Steelers and Los Angeles Rams. To watch his shredded muscle work in three 1960s-era Tarzan pics and on 70mm film was a revelation. He was a man's man who was nothing less than inspiration distilled down to its essence.

KEEPING IT ON THE DL

ROBERT: I knew from a very early age that I was different from other people and that I liked guys. I never had any desire to be intimate with a female. I really kept everything to myself. I probably did have somewhat effeminate characteristics about me, like the way I talked and acted. My exposure to gay life was extremely limited, though. I remember being frustrated, but I always kept it within me. I channeled my frustration into making art—and being good at it. I was an overachiever. I was smart and got good grades. I was president of the Honor Society. I joined the band. I was the lead in the class play. I always got appointed to committees, like, I was the chair of the committee that decorated for the senior prom. I was very active, and it kept my mind occupied and helped prevent me from sinking into a depression. I was very secretive when I was in my grade school years. I would express my homosexual tendencies by using what was available to me, which was basically *National Geographic* magazine and a Sears catalog, the men's underwear section. I would frequently thumb through the pages; then I would become aroused seeing the images of near-naked male figures.

MICK: I saw that the world had very bad things to say about people who came out as *homosexuals.* The first time that I heard the word "gay," it was equated with New York City homosexuals and the Stonewall Riots. I was only twelve years old. It was that strange time between clinging onto boyhood and adolescence. There's all this adult stuff going around that I was taking in. Extremely . . . homoerotic. I call this "the secret life of boys."

I dreaded water polo in swim class. I was small and always being crushed by the older boys or not allowed to play. There did come a change and discovery. In one iteration of water polo we played, there were no nets. A player was to swim to the other end of the pool, holding the ball in front of him, and place the ball in the opponent's end or "gutter." To score, the player had to keep the ball for fifteen seconds, holding it between himself and the pool gutter. Meanwhile the other boys would pull both player and ball away from the gutter before the coach blew his whistle. Kicking and punching were allowed.

I swam to the opposite end of the pool, treading at one of the corners. Suddenly, the ball plopped in front of me. I was excited. My heart was pounding. I placed the ball against my chest and turned around. After walking two steps in the water, I jammed the ball between me and the pool gutter. Before the others could pry me and the ball from the gutter, the coach had blown his whistle. Score!

The biggest stud in the class—Paul, six-foot, blond-haired, blue-eyed, cannonball-shouldered with ripped abs—swam up to me. In a very low voice, he said, "I don't know what you're good for, but I just love you." Paul stood up in the water. As water flowed off his large, thick, and solid slab of muscled pecs, he grabbed and held on to me really tight. After Paul released me, the coach actually congratulated me. At the end of that reporting period, he gave me the elusive grade of A. It was the only time. Paul inspired me to greatness.

JESSAY: I had a cousin who had a boyfriend whose name was Cephus. He was the most handsome man and kind to me. Girl, I was all up in his lap all the time. When I was sixteen, my dad found a letter I wrote to a boy professing my love. He knew, but he didn't know because I refused to admit it to protect myself. "I don't know what you're talking about," I lied. He didn't give up that easily. "It has your name on it," he pressed. I took out a piece of paper and wrote my name in different handwriting. I was so relieved I could do different penmanship on the spot. "Do they look alike?" I asked as calmly as possible. He conceded they didn't but then snarled, "If I find out you're a queer, I'll kill you." I knew that he meant it, so it was like, *Oh, hell no. I ain't telling this man.* He always thought I was gay, and that's why he didn't hang around with me. My sister was his son.

HOMO HONEYS, AKA "BEARDS"

BILL: I knew I had to play the straight role. It was just something I did naturally. I went to all the school dances, and I dated girls.

ROBERT: In junior high, I took a series of ballroom dancing classes, and I enjoyed dancing with females. I took a neighbor girlfriend to the senior prom.

MICK: Most of my friends in grade school and junior high were females. I got along with them very well. In fact, I liked being with girls better than boys because girls treated you better. With boys, it's always so competitive. I dated girls, but I didn't have sex with them, particularly because I didn't want to get anybody pregnant. I discovered underage drinking at the time. I came from a mining town, remember? So the drinking was epic. But drinking was also right up there with teenage pregnancies.

FINDING OUR PEOPLE

BILL: I kept my nose clean and didn't let anyone get close to me. The second I was able to legally drive a car at sixteen years old, I hightailed it down to Laguna Beach in my dad's Ford Falcon Ranchero. I was speeding down Laguna Canyon Road when I hit a soft shoulder and the car fishtailed and spun out into a field. The car was towed, and the police dropped me off downtown so I could wait for my dad there. As we walked up and down the boardwalk, I noticed a bar right next to the Hotel Laguna—there were a ton of men hanging out on the porch. I saw a lot of Speedos. I thought, *Wow, that looks like a men's club.* I did a little more research about it, and I found out, no, it wasn't a men's club, it was the gay beach. And the city founders were absolutely livid that when tourists came into town and hit the boardwalk, the first thing they saw was all of these gay guys in Speedos. The police department hired photographers from the local paper, and back then, the photographers wore a coat and tie and had the big old-fashioned cameras with giant bulbs, and they walked down the boardwalk in the heat of the sun to take pictures of the gay men to scare them away.

When that didn't work, they put up volleyball nets where the gay beach was. Well, not long after, there were gay volleyball teams and the net posts were sprayed gold and had fake ferns on top.

The men on the beach piqued my curiosity. I went to the local library, got a fake library card, and checked out books on homosexuality. I learned terms like "queen" and "chicken." I was a chicken because I was so young. Of course, there were chicken hawks, too. I started driving to Hollywood by myself, to the open-air Las Palmas Bookstand, so I could browse through the magazines. Pornography was very illegal at the time, so it was mostly muscle mags. I also went to a coffeehouse called the 8727 Club on Melrose Avenue. One time I saw a fellow student from West Covina High School there, but we didn't talk, and pretended the other didn't exist. When I went to Hollywood, it was exciting and scary. But I needed to find out more.

MICK: In my twenty-first year, the feelings for very hot-looking guys had become overwhelming. Up to then I'd had several girlfriends. I thought the road was set. I could no longer ignore the clues within myself. I got help. I attended a college outside of the Twin Cities— Minneapolis and St. Paul. By chance I'd met a licensed psychologist in the city and made an appointment to see him. He set me right on some things. I'd thought that all gay people were either pedophiles or drag queens. In therapy, he said that most pedophiles are not gay. Dressing up in drag was a cultural thing. American men have deep fears of being seen as the opposite of masculine, refusing to acknowledge and show their feminine side. Perceptions were gelling together because I was coming out and discovering my unique identity. Never had I considered that the dislike toward me had to do with my sexual identity. By now, I'd come to the decision that if I was going to have a life lived openly, it would have to be in another place. One where I could meet other gay men. In the late 1970s, that meant the coasts.

By fate or intervention, I chose Southern California. Before color television, on January 1, I would watch the Rose Parade and game. I'd imagined myself being on the beach, getting some color of my own, eighty-degree weather, and surrounded by big, muscled guys.

JESSAY: In college in Tennessee, I snuck out my dorm window to go to the one drag bar in town. Once I ran into a ministry student, and when I said hi to him, he looked terrified. "I'm not supposed to be here," he whispered. "I'm not either," I told him. "And I'm not going to tell on you." I didn't go out when I was on the road. I met gay people, but it was at the concert. I discovered gay bars like Embers in Portland in the early '80s because of a straight friend of mine at work, Vanelda. She was a cute little thing. We would go out on Thursday nights after work and just dance and dance. It was good, clean fun. She was my gal. I also liked Darcelle XV, a bar owned by this lesbian whose ex-husband I kind of dipped and dabbed with. Of course, if I was going out to dance with a girl, I wasn't going to be looking for anybody. I wasn't one of those who go, "I'll see you later," and ditch my friend for a hookup. I honestly was just there to dance. Walking into a gay bar in the '80s was intimidating. I never approached a guy; they had to come speak to me first. I'm still that way.

ROBERT: I left Arkansas and headed to Washington University in St. Louis to study architecture. I learned where the few gay bars were located, like Peyton Place, which was located in a now-defunct entertainment district known as Gaslight Square. It had a back door in the back alley. After many drive-bys and deliberations, I finally decided it was safe to check out. The first few times I was so scared. I'd walk in and mainly observe what was going on by myself. Eventually, I did start talking to people and occasionally hooking up. I became friendly with a popular bartender/drag queen named Tony who, a few years later, became a tenant in one of my apartment buildings. My second year, I learned about gay cruising taking place in Forest Park, which was right next to the university. I drove around looking for it and finally found it. It was through park cruising that I actually started having my first real sexual experiences.

6

OLD FLAMERS

First Times and Not-So-Easy Lovers

V-CARD STAMPED

ROBERT: By the time I got to around seventh grade, I began having sleepovers with guys who I was attracted to. For the most part they were pretty innocent—initially there was no physical contact. It was just the camaraderie of being with another guy my age. But two resulted in sexual experiences. My first ever was a real cute guy by the name of Jimmy John Dale.* He had three first names like a good Southern boy. I couldn't take my eyes off him. We developed

---

* Names have been changed to protect the innocent . . . and not-so-innocent.

a friendship, and I invited him over. We only had a two-bedroom house. Mom and Dad slept in one bedroom, and all three boys slept in the other bedroom. We had a fold-out sofa in the living room, and that's where it all went down. The house was so small, so I do not see how it was physically possible that my mom and dad and brothers didn't know what happened, but they never said a thing to me. It was almost like it was accepted, but not talked about.

JESSAY: My first kiss was with my pastor's son when I was seven. He was two years older. I don't get how people get guilty after doing something they've enjoyed. I was a pro at seven! I was comfortable with everything. It was just natural to me. My main thing was learning how to kiss. As a kid, I would apply Vaseline and kiss the mirror and make sure it looked right. It had to be perfect. I had crushes on all the guys in my hometown. And the thing is, I had sex with almost all of my friends, real straight guys. It boggled my mind for quite some time. Like, how can they do this and then leave me for girls?

BILL: My first time happened in Laguna Beach. As soon as I plunked down, I was picked up right away. I wanted to jump in! The first time I went to bed with a man, I felt so much guilt and shame because I'd been told all my life that it was wrong. I just went ahead and did it anyway. I really felt low. Really low.

When Your "First" Time Comes from Abuse

MICK: My first sexual experience was at the age of eight, and that was with my father's best friend. My abuser was an alcoholic, he was an anti-Semitic, homophobic, misogynist, racist, straight, white, linebacker size of a man. He had a ranch outside of my hometown where he kept horses. He used to give rides to all of us kids. He also had two sons.

I can only speak for myself here. Finny took me for a ride through a wooded area on the ranch. We stopped in the middle of a trail. It was windy, gray, and cold. I was seated in the saddle in front of him. It was then that he pulled down my pants. At age eight, I did not know what was taking place. What I remember saying is, "Uncle Finny, oh! It burns! It burns! Stop! Stop! Stop!" I was crying. Because I'd kept crying and making noise he eventually stopped. After that I was disinvited to the ranch. Finny explained to my dad, "Your boy cries so much."

This drama/trauma hasn't been too bad for me. Firsthand, I do know that his other victims struggled their entire lives after he'd assaulted them. The way I looked at my situation? Finny was just the first of many men to follow in life. Let me be clear: he did not make me gay. I did question why I was so promiscuous, though. Research and studies suggest that this may be a result of having been abused. As they say, "It's the only love you know."

Look, I've forgiven Finny for his actions and behavior. In public, he was always nice to me and treated me fairly. Having been excluded from his ranch was a good thing.

....

OUR FIRST LOVES

Bill's Sugar Daddy

My mom always rented a vacation house at either Balboa Island or Laguna Beach for the family during the summer. When I was twenty, my mom said, "Bill, go find us a house." I drove down to Laguna, walked into the first real estate office I saw, and met a tall, dark-haired, handsome broker named John. He had a Cesar Romero–type look. He asked me if I wanted a cup of coffee and who was I to deny. John and I sat and chatted for a long time. "Come back anytime," he said when I left.

Well, when we hit the beach for summer vacation, I went to a party, and randomly John was there. We talked all night. In fact, he was the only one I talked to the entire evening. He was much older than me, forty-five, and had just broken up with his partner of ten years, who was a songwriter for Disney. John, who apparently had been dating younger guys after his split, invited me to dinner the next night. We had a drink in his oceanfront house and watched the sun go, then headed to a restaurant on the water called Berkshires in Newport Beach. It was so romantic, and he wined and dined me. We feasted on shrimp cocktail, Chateaubriand, and a Grand Marnier soufflé for dessert, and drank a Château Lafite Rothschild. It was absolutely exquisite.

The very next night he took me to dinner again and things really started to get serious. Two months later, I moved in with him! We pretended I was one of his property managers. He had a guesthouse, a little shack underneath the house, which we turned into a fake bedroom for me in case anyone asked. That's where I pretended that I slept. I very quickly had a sugar daddy, and it was wonderful . . . at first.

John really wooed me. I was starting school at Orange Coast College, so he bought me brand-new clothes. He absolutely knew the way to my heart. He flew me to San Francisco for fabulous dinners at Nob Hill hot spot Alexis' Tangier, which had a strolling violin player. They brought us the special wine list, which I immediately opened and pointed at a 1947 Château Lafite Rothschild. "Order it," John said. It was $125 in 1964, which is like $1,000 today. He put me on a pedestal and was throwing gifts and dinners at me.

John swept me off my feet. I kind of didn't know what was happening to me. He introduced me to A-list society. We were invited to fancy cocktail parties in Bel Air at Don Loper's house. Don, a famous costume designer for the likes of Ella Fitzgerald, took an immediate liking to us, and we spent weekends at his mansion. He was a witty, entertaining, grand queen who knew almost everyone in Hollywood. He had black-tie dinner parties for ten at a large round draped table.

I met the then-editor of *Architectural Digest*, Bradley Little. I met famous Broadway producer Gant Gaither, who was besties with Princess Grace. Don had three staff, and when the plates were brought out from the kitchen, he had to approve them before they were brought to the guest. He was always very formal and wore black suits exclusively with a small red rose boutonniere attached to his lapel. He had a vintage Mercedes-Benz, and in the back were a pair of Waterford bud vases that held a small bouquet of miniature red roses. One weekend we all got in the limousine and headed to the Brown Derby for lunch. He always sat in the booth where the caricature of him was prominently displayed.

John and I had some really good times together. We lasted about ten months, from September through July. We broke up because of two things. One, my dad made a surprise visit to the beach one afternoon and caught us off guard. He barely knocked before walking into the living room. He immediately saw a giant oil portrait John was painting of me and that I was naked from the waist up. That caused a bit of a hullabaloo. He took one look, turned around with a disgusted look on his face, and stormed out. He wasn't even there more than ten minutes; he'd just wanted to spy on me. My dad and I never discussed the incident.

The other issue was that John had some serious problems. He made two suicide attempts while I was living with him. I was only twenty-one, and dealing with someone with such mature problems was a turnoff, to say the least. Not only was John unstable, I found out later that he was having a financial crisis. I left John three months after my dad's surprise visit. Not long after that, I found out John married his twenty-four-year-old female Hungarian housekeeper. Some people just can't be alone.

Jessay's Long-Distance Lover

Even though I'd had sex with boys my age growing up, marriage was a foreign thing I knew I couldn't have. But I was weak. I lusted after men. I knew I liked dick. One summer after college, I was in Orlando visiting with a friend, and we had a conversation about relationships. I said, "It's impossible for two men to fall in love; it's just sex." That evening, we went to a bar called Parliament House. We were having cocktails, when a six-foot-four-inch hunk of chocolate came up behind me.

"Excuse me, would you like to dance?" a thunderous voice boomed in my ear.

I turned around, looked up, and there he was. Samuel Coleman Washington III. I melted.

We danced and talked and had an immediate connection. I spent the night at his place, then went back to Miami, where I was living at the time. The following week, I invited him to my birthday party, and, to my delight, he drove down for it. We were an item from that moment on. Samuel Coleman Washington III was the first man that I ever loved.

A month after we met, in August 1977, I had to go on the road for my first tour ever as a professional singer with a group called Harvest Celebration, a brand-new contemporary gospel group. Our home base was going to be in Lincoln, Nebraska, and I had to move there. I was willing to give it up for love. "No way," Samuel said. "I do not want that on you, that you didn't live the life you wanted because of me."

"Love does that," I argued.

"No, you need to go."

So, we dated long distance for five years, eleven months out of the year. Every time I was off, I would go to him in Orlando. Eventually, we started drifting apart, plus we were very different people. Samuel didn't like white people, but it was because he didn't know any. Whites were the enemies. When we got together, he had to change his attitude, because I told him I got everybody in my world. Yeah. I'm not losing my friends. They were here before you got here. And they will be here when you leave.

We broke up, mostly because I was always on the road touring, but we remained friends. Sadly, about five years after we split, Samuel died from AIDS.

Mick's Muscle Man

After graduation from Gustavus Adolphus College in Minnesota, I moved to Southern California. I loaded up a Chevrolet Vega with possessions I thought I was going to need—like a pair of downhill skis and a secondhand hard copy of *The Annotated Works of William Shakespeare*. When I got to Des Moines, I turned right on Interstate 80, heading west. By the time I got to Utah it was the following night. The interstate follows the south shore of Salt Lake. It was ninety degrees, so the windows were open. The air was hot and briny. On the AM radio, the only station with a clear and loud signal was KNX News Radio Los Angeles. During the early hours, the station would air a vintage recording of a radio play taken from the CBS archive. I recall hearing for the first time an over-the-air advert with copy that to this day has never been altered or changed. It is for a car showroom located at Olympic and Bundy Streets in West LA. I thought that sounded so exotic and sophisticated, hearing over the roar of my Chevrolet Vega engine, electrified in the crisp briny air of the Great Salt Lake, a disembodied basso melodic voice utter the immortal words: "Olympic at Bundy . . . in West Los Angeles."

In Laguna Beach, I found a two-bedroom house to share with a gay-friendly guy named Ken. Perched on the top of Aliso Canyon Road, our magnificent view west over the ocean extended as far as the Santa Catalina Islands. Over the next six months, I hooked up with a lot of guys. A free sexual life! Finally away from all that I had known before.

Late one winter's afternoon, after returning from class and entering the house, Ken called down to me from the upstairs living room. "Michael!" (I was not Mick in those days.) "Come upstairs—I want you to meet somebody."

I walked up the stairs. Sitting on the couch there was a five-foot-four bodybuilder from England, John Tristram. A former Mr. Olympia. I recognized him immediately. John had introduced himself to me at the gay beach in South Laguna the previous summer. I thought we didn't hit it off. For an hour I'd sat in my Vega with no air-conditioning, crying because I felt so terrible that I had blown it with one of my idols.

Turns out, John felt a spark and had tracked me down. Not only did we fall in love, John changed my life in so many ways. After a hard training where he taught me professional-level bodybuilding, we'd get stoned and have athletic, heart-pumping, long sessions of raw sex. The following summer, in 1979, he took me to my first gay pride parade. That year the parade had moved to then-unincorporated West Hollywood. The parade lasted two blocks on Santa Monica Boulevard, from San Vicente to Robertson. At Santa Monica and San Vicente, the sheriff's station was newly completed. The fair was held on an asphalt parking lot between the station and the also newly constructed Blue Whale building of the Pacific Design Center, the same lot on which the Red and Green Buildings along with the fountain and art gallery buildings now stand. My first gay pride parade was a revelation. Not for its floats or moving entrants, like Parents and Friends of Lesbians and Gays, but for the bare, big, cut and muscled, hairy- and smooth-chested, and distressed-blue-jean-clad studs.

John often drove me in his Volvo station wagon to Gold's Gym in Venice to train. That's when he introduced me to legendary body-builders like Chris Dickerson and Jim French, the genius behind *Colt* magazine. John had modeled for Mr. French. Because he was a teacher (French language) in the LA public schools and an instructor at UCLA, John did not want his face shown in any of Mr. French's photos. Yet I can pick out John's body in any Jim French/*Colt* magazine pictures. He was well-endowed. An experienced top, five-foot-four, incredibly muscular, and with tree-trunk-sized quadriceps/hamstrings. In so many ways, John Tristram was my dream muscle daddy lover.

The only thing was that John wasn't connected directly with the industry . . . show business. I wanted that so much, too. I was enrolled into the Graduate School of Fine Arts at UC Irvine. Being an actor was going to be my life's work. Little did I realize how difficult this path would turn out to be . . .

John was twice my age. He'd discovered bodybuilding because he'd suffered from rickets as a child, during the extremely lean war years (WWII) spent in England. After leaving the British Merchant Marine and time spent in NYC, at last he'd disembarked at Los Angeles, in time to fully participate at Muscle Beach during its zenith. In this laboratory of "better living through chemistry," he transformed his weakened body into a specimen—in my opinion an achievement worthy of admiration and personal inspiration. After John's death I inherited his custom-made, durable, and soft-to-the-touch leather weight belt.

John was of the Silent Generation. He was a schoolteacher, and he hid his sexual identity. I do think about the path not chosen. John and I were together for six months—at that time, an eternity in gay years.

Robert's Move-in-Ready Rendezvous

I met my first lover in the art and architectural library at Washington University in my fourth year. Mike was a brilliant man. He was a student, too, there on a National Science Foundation grant and in his third year doing his PhD in physical chemistry. After he graduated, he got a job as a research chemist in a small St. Louis chemical company and later became a chief research chemist for Monsanto Chemical Corporation, doing laboratory experiments, literally creating matter. I had seen him before on campus and thought he was so handsome. He was a dark-haired Italian with a small, muscular body frame, like a gymnast. We struck up a whispered conversation in the library, and before you knew it, we were roommates.

For several months, we didn't touch each other. Then we were invited to visit a friend who had tickets to the Indianapolis 500 auto race. We ended up sleeping in the same bed on the trip, and we made first contact. That opened the door for the sexual part of our relationship. I'd had crushes on guys before that, but either it couldn't go anywhere because it was a celebrity-type crush that would never happen anyway, or it didn't go anywhere because the conditions just weren't right. This was the first time I'd had an emotional and sexual connection with a man.

Back at home, we started sharing the same bed, so that was a pretty radical change. Pretty soon we decided we needed more space as a couple, and we learned about a carriage house in a lovely neighborhood. The carriage house was located over the three-car garage of a mansion on one of the private streets built near Forest Park around the time of the 1904 World's Fair. The house was owned by one of the professors at the university's medical school. The rent was a little above our budget, but we worked out a deal to do yard duties in exchange for living there.

Eventually, we grew out of that space, too, so in 1969 we moved into an apartment in a six-unit building on Buckingham Court. Just a few months later, out of the blue, the owner asked us if we'd be interested in buying the building. We scraped together the $8,000 down payment, with the help of a straight lawyer friend of Mike's. By the late '70s, the three of us together owned thirteen buildings with 365 apartment units and sixty thousand square feet of commercial space. We built a real estate empire valued at more than $6 million, generating over a million per year income for our partnership.

Mike and I were in a monogamous relationship for seven years. We were living the high life. We drove matching Jaguars and traveled a lot—frequent road trips to Chicago, New York, and Provincetown on Cape Cod, plus at least one annual vacation to Europe. He was very rational about everything, very even-tempered, analytical, and quiet, so we developed a very cerebral relationship. It was a pretty nice life.

There was one major problem, however. Our relationship was not intensely sexual. It was more about two guys living together and working together. I wasn't getting everything that I apparently wanted sexually, so after a few years, I started doing my own thing. Mike never probed or showed any element of jealousy. It was almost like I could do what I wanted, and it was okay with him. I found a cruising park on Confederate Circle in Forest Park, of all places, and that's where I met Chris. He was much younger than me and looked like Joe Namath. He was into horses, so he spent a lot of time going to stables and riding all day and chumming around with people like the Anheuser-Busch family at horse shows. Chris tried to get me to ride, but I was too much of a sissy. I mean, for me, it's a long way to the ground from the back of that horse.

Only a few months after we met, Mike came home one day and caught Chris and me in a compromising position. Mike just turned around and left without saying anything. Soon Mike fell into a serious relationship with another friend of ours, named Bill, who it turned out he'd been dallying with on the side during our relationship. They're still together to this day, fifty years later. Mike and Bill and Chris and I lived in the same apartment building for a year. How very lesbian of us!

Chris and I developed an intensely sexual relationship. Once given the opportunity, I wanted to know and experiment more. Chris provided the sexual energy that I was looking for. Nothing too extreme, no leather or bondage, just more spicy. I had my first three-way when I was with Chris.

Chris and I dated for the next seven years, but a lot of friction started to develop between us. A part of that had to do with Chris seeing other people. Unlike Mike, I was the jealous type, so I flipped out when Chris cheated. After we broke up, Chris taunted me. He would come by my house with another guy in tow, showing off. That was the straw that broke the camel's back. I moved out of my apartment and moved out of St. Louis. I headed for the gay Mecca—San Francisco.

SITUATIONSHIPS AND OTHER STICKY SITUATIONS

Bill's High-Society Honey

I moved up to Northern California to get space from my dad and landed a job managing a high-end men's clothing store in Los Gatos.

One well-dressed, extremely handsome gentleman kept coming in to see me, and one day, invited me out to lunch. Michael McGuire was an absolute charmer. He was drop-dead gorgeous and looked like John Saxon. Lucky me, he was very wealthy, a trust-fund baby from Chicago. His grandfather helped develop the tugboat system on Lake Michigan in Chicago. The McGuire family had eight children, and one was as good-looking as the next. Michael's brother John was in an ad for *Playboy* magazine, and his mother was a debutante and society star. She was so gorgeous the Chicago newspapers nicknamed her "Angel Puss." He was extremely close to his mother.

The McGuires had connections all over town, so it was a thrill to go to Chicago with Michael. They had memberships at the White Hall Club and the Standard Club. We stayed at the Drake and dined at the Ambassador East. At the world-famous Pump Room, we sat in booth number one. I saw the best of everything in that city.

Michael expected the best—after all, he was born with a silver spoon in his mouth—and I bent over backward to please him. He loved my cooking but had one rule: if there wasn't a sauce on the entree, there had to be two sauces on the dessert. We both loved the finer things in life, but there was one problem. He had tons of money, and I didn't. When I first started dating Michael, I opened an antiques showroom in the SOMA neighborhood of San Francisco. Michael bought a bookstore, but he didn't have a head for business, he just looked pretty.

I loved being on Michael's arm. He was so handsome and well-mannered, and we rarely argued. There was no door-slamming during fights. It was all very classy and civil. We had the same values, and we had a lot in common. We both loved the good life and going out for romantic dinners. But he had some issues that were dealbreakers for me. For one, he was extremely cheap. He definitely wasn't as generous as my previous sugar daddy, who spoiled me rotten and showered me with gifts. Michael always wanted to go to Trader Vic's for dinner, but I had just started a business. It was an instant success but not flush with cash. "Michael, you know I'm tight," I'd say.

"I'll loan you the money," he'd respond.

Another time he wanted to go to Puerto Vallarta, so he just up and went to Mexico, and left me at home.

Michael also got heavy into drugs. At that time, cocaine was everywhere. So he got kind of weird, and our relationship lost a lot of its luster. People said, "Well, you're his cook and house cleaner, what else could he want?" I decided I wanted more, and it was time to move on. We'd been together for five years, and in early 1972 we decided to split up. Our breakup was mutual and amicable. I found an apartment in the Pacific Heights neighborhood of San Francisco and was single for the next eight years. Michael got wilder and wilder. Ultimately, we drifted apart and lost touch.

A couple of years ago, I decided to google the McGuires in Chicago. Doing my research, I found the obituary for Angel Puss. As I was reading, I stopped cold. It said, "Carlotta was preceded in death by her son Michael." She adored him, and I did, too. I cared for Michael, and I loved him.

Jessay's Live-In Lover

In 1981, my last year on the road touring, I joined an organization called Seventh-day Adventist Kinship International, which I'm still a member of. It's a gay support group, and it saved my life because I found out I wasn't alone. There were other Christian gay people. The organization had a newsletter, and I was first introduced to it on the road from an old college friend, who I had no idea was gay. He came up to me at a church in Scottsdale, Arizona, and gave me this newspaper, and said, "Don't read it now. You're gonna get in trouble." And, of course, I ran to the bus and opened it right up. People were watching me, but I didn't care. I needed this. I felt so alone all those years. I still wasn't out. I was flaming and didn't even know it. But my mom was totally oblivious to it all. That's what tickled me to death.

After years on the road, I needed to settle down and get a place. I wanted to go to a town where nobody knew me or that I sang. I wanted to make friends, just being authentically me, not being "Jessay the

Singer." I chose Vancouver, Washington, "the bedroom of Portland," I called it.

I continued going to support group meetings through Seventh-day Adventist Kinship International. And that is where I met Dusty, the first lover I ever lived with. He was Caucasian and adopted into his family. He had this "left behind" complex because his mom literally left him on the steps of a house. So he had that fear of being left and always tried to keep me under him. I didn't know any better at the age of twenty-seven.

Because of my innocence, I didn't realize that he was taking advantage of me. I said, "Well, let me go out and find a job and stuff." So I would go out and hunt around and tell him about the job, all excited. Nothing was ever good enough for me.

Dusty and I were together for two years before he suggested that I should try living by myself. I was actually excited to pay bills. Because they were mine. One day, Dusty came over and, seeing how well I was doing on my own, said, "Are you ready to come back home?"

"I am home. I'm not coming back."

That's when the anger started. "I'm gonna tell everybody in the church that you're gay," he threatened.

"All you're gonna do is hurt yourself," I replied calmly. "We've been going there together all this time. You don't think they know?" I shut the fire down. I was so cool. I was so proud of myself.

The last time I saw Dusty was at one of the Kinship camp meetings in Oregon at this beautiful campground. We spoke cordially to each other, and I haven't seen him since. I have no idea where he is, if he's dead or if he's alive.

Mick's Initiation into SoCal Man Sex

To paraphrase from the lyrics of "I Love L.A." (Randy Newman), "Look at these *men*, ain't nothing like 'em nowhere." I had so much fun when I was single in Southern California. The first year I lived in Laguna Beach atop Aliso Canyon Road. We used to have great parties because our house was in South Laguna, like two blocks up from the beach. We called our place the "Swish Alps." I started to wear Speedo swimsuits, and my body was fit. I really started to cut up at that time. I would walk down to the beach in front of the Boom Boom Room showing off my goods. I dated a model named John McMurray, who was supposedly one of the Shah of Iran's rent boys. And lots of marines because the Camp Pendleton Base was right there. These guys were six-foot-three, really muscular. I gravitated to them.

OUR COMING-OUT STORIES

Jessay wrote his mom a letter

One of my favorite childhood memories is when a teacher of mine named Ms. Jones informed my mom that I was always surrounded by girls on the playground, and they giggled about it and wondered which one of them I'd end up marrying.

I don't know how this is possible, but nobody in my family was sure I was gay—except, of course, for my dad, who saw all the sissy stuff I did and threatened to kill me if I ever came out as queer. I knew that he meant it. So I was like, *Aw, hell no. I ain't telling this man.* So he knew but he didn't *know*. I refused to admit it.

It's pretty shocking that my mom didn't know I was gay from day one. I was her baby and she didn't think anything about it. She was just raising me and letting me be me. She was there for me all the time. Even when I was being a sissy. I didn't realize I was being a sissy then, but looking back, going through old pictures, everything was a head tilt. I laugh now and go, "Look at me! I'm prettier than the girls!" But I loved playing my sports, too. I was a well-rounded gay guy. I remember I wanted to play football. I was in one game, but when my mom saw all the boys pile up on me, she said no more and literally ran over and retrieved me from the scrum and took me home. She embarrassed me in front of my high school class. I'm sure I was enjoying it more than it looked.

My sister Aubrey should have known I was gay. I was a horny little boy, and I had sex a lot at our house starting at the age of seven with boys my own age. She was our lookout, always telling us when mom was coming home, so my paramour could escape out the window. But in college she got really mad at me because some guy outed me to her. She was upset because I hadn't told her I was gay myself first. She wanted specifically to hear it from me instead of a friend of mine who told her. I hadn't even thought about coming out to her because I thought she knew. I couldn't figure out why she was so angry at me all the time, so I finally asked her why. She finally admitted, "You didn't tell me you were gay."

"I thought you knew," I said. "What'd you think I was doing all those times you were being the lookout? Doing my nails?"

"Well, I knew what you were doing, but it was just boys being boys."

"No, it wasn't just 'boys being boys' for me." So we had a little rift there because I had no idea why she didn't want to speak to me. And that was why. I hadn't spoken the word. I realized I had to speak it; it couldn't just be implied. I was totally caught off guard by that, but we got past it really quickly, and it taught me a valuable lesson. She wasn't mad that I was gay, she was mad that I hadn't been honest with her. It felt like a lie because of omission. Once it was all out in the open, we were fine.

Between fear of my father and my full immersion in the church world, I kept my sexual proclivities to myself for a long time, which probably confused my mom and my sister. In 1972, when I was nineteen years old, my dad died. I will never forget the feeling that washed over me at his funeral. That was the moment I said to myself, "I'm free." People kept commenting about how happy I looked. The only thing I could muster in response was, "He's at peace now." That's all I said.

After my dad died, I really started living authentically. I was finally comfortable with myself. I never made a big sweeping announcement about being gay, because that wasn't my style. My new philosophy became, when somebody asks, I will always say yes. I felt if they were brave enough to bring it up, they were pretty much ready to know the truth. They just needed to hear you say it, from your lips to God's ears.

My mom did not get to the point of asking me herself on her own. She kept asking me, "When are you going to get married?" You know, like all parents do. When I was twenty-eight, I moved in with Dusty, my first boyfriend, in Vancouver, Washington. My sister, at that point, knew I was gay, and I felt like I couldn't keep lying to my mother, who I absolutely adored. I was like, *Ooh, I gotta put this news out there.* So I wrote my mom an emotional letter and asked my sister and brother-in-law to read it with her. That's how I did it. I had no doubt that she would continue loving me, but I couldn't handle the hurt. My mom read the letter, and it was smooth. She cried because she felt that she'd left me alone all those years and she wasn't there to help me. And I reminded her, "Mom, you're in church. You probably would've sent me to one of those camps that would've electrocuted me or something." She said, "Oh my goodness, you're probably right. How horrible." She admitted she was totally oblivious to my flaming propensities. And that's when I showed her some picture poses of me as a kid. You know, "Hello?" We had a good laugh about it.

My mom was very accepting of Dusty, aka "my two-year headache." She thought he was very feminine, and his mannerisms were flamboyant. I never noticed it until she said it. Then my immediate thought was, *Oh my God, he's cuter than me.*

"That's who he is," I stated, and from that moment on, when we talked, she'd say, "I love you and I love him. You tell him that I love him and look forward to meeting him." It was the easiest thing. The hardest part was me telling her, because I didn't want to hurt her. After that she just became this advocate for gays, period. Nobody was allowed to say anything about anybody around her. She also felt comfortable enough to reveal her own secret to me. "I have something to tell you," she said mysteriously.

"Uh-oh. Don't tell me you're a lesbian at this late stage. No, girl, we can only have one gay in the family."

"Oh no." She laughed. She was excited to tell me that she once had a "homosexual" roommate before she met my dad. That's when I educated her not to say that word again. I said, "Your faith drops when you say 'homosexual'; just say 'gay' and you're happy." Well, anyway, she had a gay roommate, and she would protect him from people. She allowed nobody to say anything bad to him, which surprised me. Not that she was so caring, but that she'd had a gay roommate. In my mind, we were even!

After I came out, my mom was pure love. Because that's who she always was. I'm like her; she's like me. We love the world. We come in with open arms. That's what she did for Dusty, too, then Don, my late partner of ten years. She was there for us when he was dying. I wish the world could have met that woman. She was my ally, my heart, my protector. My mom's been gone ten years now, and I really miss her.

Robert's family motto was "Don't ask, don't tell"

Coming out was a slow process for me.

My parents always accepted me for who I was, but it wasn't overt. We were from Arkansas, after all. My whole upbringing was based around a few very simple rules, if you will. Some of those rules being what you don't talk about—especially sex, politics, and religion. Because if you did talk about them, you were going to end up alienating people or getting into arguments. Nowadays, everyone talks about everything, and not surprisingly, we've never been more divided.

Anyhoo, during my second year of college in St. Louis, my father died at the age of fifty from a massive stroke. From that point on, my mom was the only parent that I was relating to. When I met my first boyfriend, Mike, in 1965, my mom came to St. Louis, and we all went to dinner a number of times. She knew we lived together but never asked me anything about it. She just made comments to me like, "Mike is such a nice guy." Mom always accepted Mike and it felt good. I think subconsciously it helped me come out.

Now, I wasn't really all that comfortable with my sexuality myself until I was about twenty-three. In my pre-college school years, I did start getting together with guys and having sexual experiences with them. Not a lot, but a few. It felt natural, and I never felt pressure, like I had to change my feelings. It was more I had this longing and urge to find out more. I really was very much alone fighting this battle, trying to find my identity and figure out how to deal with myself in the world. I wasn't scared to explore my sexuality; I'd call it being cautious. During my early ages, there was nothing out there supporting the gay lifestyle, which might have caused me to make major moves. So it was a very gradual process. I'd take a very small step and see how that felt, and then I'd take another small step. It took me a long time to travel that journey.

One of the steps included surrounding myself with "chosen family." That means other gay people who made me feel unconditionally loved and supported. Mike and I started developing a network of friends who were gay. We went to nightclubs and had parties with small groups of people, who became extended family. But it wasn't until I moved to San Francisco, after I'd broken up with both Mike and Chris and I was on my own, when I really started developing deep friendships with people, male and female. Several of those friendships continue today. And when I made the decision to move to the desert in the late '80s, I pretty quickly developed a few really close friends who became family. People I would meet, who I would work with, who I had a good chemistry with.

Chosen family can be a lifesaver for LGBTQ+ people who feel ostracized or misunderstood by their blood family. To this day, I've never spoken to my brothers about my being gay, and I haven't seen them since my mother's funeral twenty-odd years ago. I don't see how they couldn't know.

I will say, in the '80s, when I was living in San Francisco, my older brother was a career FBI agent. And I do remember a conversation with him one time where he went out of his way to make a comment about how he had to, every once in a while, interview homosexuals on different cases. He distinctly made the comment that they were always very cooperative and nice. I felt like he was telling me at that point in time that he knew I was gay. And his experience with gays was always positive. But he didn't just come right out and say it.

I've never been upset about the absence of a close relationship with my brothers. I never really thought about it. It never bothered me. I was able to find people who accepted me and wanted to know me, gay or not.

Some say being out in the '60s was brave. At the time, I really didn't think that much about it. I just did what I felt was right for me. I've had an attitude since I was a child that I am who I am, I'm going to be who I am, and I'm not going to worry about it. My friends emboldened me. Accumulating real estate and becoming prosperous emboldened me. By the mid-'70s, I was a fighter. I never did any kind of demonstrations or anything like that, I just fought my personal battles, which were simultaneously gay rights battles. I started developing a fierceness and determination that I was going to be who I am. And if anybody didn't like it, they better get out of my way.

Bill became a member of "the Sisterhood"

The truth of the matter is, I don't have a coming-out story. I never came out to my family. I know they knew I was gay, but it was never talked about. I had no classmates to talk to or anything. My only goal when I was younger and still living at home was to prevent anyone from knowing my secret. I had to keep on my toes and watch myself. I was completely on my own figuring it out. That part was rough.

Please don't feel bad for me, though. To say, "Aw, that's so sad," doesn't really fit my narrative. Because the minute I moved from Laguna Beach up to Northern California, I was as free as a bird. I could do anything I wanted, and I didn't have to watch my p's and q's.

When I moved to Northern California, I didn't care what anyone thought of me—I was Bill, and I was going to be Bill. I no longer had any kind of restrictions around me.

It was the most exciting time of my life. I was twenty-one years old, sharing an apartment with a guy, who became a friends-with-benefits kind of a thing. We had a wild, loyal circle of gay friends we literally called "the Sisterhood." Because we were all sisters—we were all in this together. It was 1965 and gay life was not as acceptable as it is now. So we had our parties and hit the one LGBTQ+ bar in San Jose, the Crystal Café, walking down West San Fernando together as a happy and gay little gang. Inside, dykes, gay guys, and queer students from nearby San Jose State mingled until the wee hours. This was the place where I saw my first lesbian bar fight—and boy, those bra straps were snapping that night! I just absolutely loved my independence and my new chosen family. We were a tight group of guys who bonded and had the same values. We had a closeness and openness I'd never experienced with anyone back home.

That doesn't mean I didn't love my family back in Laguna. I did, very much. Everyone knew I was gay and accepted it (excluding my father), even if we didn't discuss it. My younger brother John and I were as tight as we could be growing up. My next sibling wasn't born until six years later, so John and I did everything together. Then he started to go the sports direction and I the ballet route, and we drifted a bit. I think he always knew, but he never said anything.

My mom knew what was going on, but it was one of those "let's not embarrass each other" things, like, if it's not upsetting anybody why bother bringing it out into the open? Being the nonjudgmental person she was, she never asked me questions about it. We never once had a conversation about my being gay. I referred to things, but there was never any sit-down like, *Well, Bill, what does it feel like?* I know that sounds kind of weird. But that's the way it was back then. It was rare to be out to anyone, especially your family. You were more likely to be estranged, or everyone pretended not to know or care, even if they did.

My mom and I were very close, and my being gay didn't change that one bit. Don't tell anyone, but I was her favorite. After she divorced my dad, we loved to do things together. When I was living up north, I'd always come down every year for the holidays and, for our shared birthday, May 5, we made a habit of going to the Hotel Bel-Air for a fancy lunch. Down the road, I began to be bold enough to bring my boyfriends and partners home, and she welcomed us with open arms . . . and separate bedrooms. Mom had a rule, and she stuck with it, whether her guests were straight or gay. She made my uncle and his girlfriend stay in separate bedrooms because they weren't married yet.

My father was the only one in my family who never came around about my sexuality. You'd think he'd eventually be understanding about me being gay, but no. He was fixated on proving I was a homo, and I, stubbornly and spitefully, was not about to let the cat out of the bag at all to prove him right.

Once, when I was the manager of the men's clothing store in San Jose, he came up to visit and waltzed into my job unannounced. This was around 1967.

"How are you doing?" he asked me.

"I'm doing great," I responded.

"Well, you better be," he said, "because, you know, your sexual practices aren't quite the norm."

I just thought, *Why come all the way up here and say this to me?* The underlying message was, you better watch yourself, you're going to be in trouble. I mean, here I was, I moved to Northern California alone, I got a job instantly, I was promoted to manager, and he's coming and telling me my sexual practices are going to keep me from winning? I think not, Pops.

The irony was that my father was a great showman, but *he* was the lousy businessman, not me. After he split with my mom, he married his bookkeeper, who it turned out was very fond of alcohol. His life went downhill from there. He and his new wife ended up losing the restaurant because they owed thousands in back taxes. They were forced to sell her home and move into a trailer. Then they ran out of money completely, and my sister, brother, and I committed to giving them $100 per month each.

One Christmas I came down to visit him, and I was just appalled to see how bad my father looked. He was disheveled and his hair was a mess. So I took him in the bathroom, sat him down, got some shears, and cut his hair. In the end, I felt sorry for him. Yes, he'd been horrible to me, but he was still my father. We are all human—whether straight, gay, or anything in between—and we need to judge each other less and appreciate each other's differences more.

Mick moved out and came out

Of the four of us, I'm the most liberated. I have no shame about this. I've been on my own since I was eighteen. I was twenty-two when I came out in my senior year of college. By the time I was twenty-four, my whole family knew. That doesn't mean that my coming out was seamless or easy, per se, just earlier than most.

I was in Minneapolis, a city with a large gay population, during the summer between my junior and senior years. There were bars along Hennepin Avenue, including a country and western hole that had a following among the Lacoste-polo-shirt-and-penny-loafer set. It was in nearby St. Paul where I met a psychologist who helped me overcome my fears and to accept, celebrate, and embrace my bisexual identity. Unfortunately, there was pushback at college that senior year. Resistance along with a fair amount of pettiness came forth from classmates. Could they have been struggling with the same issues?

On the other hand, my professors were very supportive. They cautioned me that homophobia was a fact of show business. One professor was a really cool guy. He was gay, too. He introduced me to his circle of gay colleagues and friends. But he, too, warned me, saying, "You have to be careful. You have to make decisions about persona and privacy. There will be testing of your resolve. You've chosen to be out of the mainstream of society. What does that mean for your life?" It meant that the path was going to be tough . . . probably.

That year I came out to my older sister Carolyn. She was the first of my family to know. "Well, I'm glad that you decided on your sexual identity," she said nonchalantly. "Can we move on?" It really didn't matter to her.

I'd come out to the rest of my family after moving to California. They were thousands of miles away. Out of sight, out of mind. Me, I was busy enjoying newfound independence, the sunshine, and sex. I was living a far more open life. There was an ebbing concern as to my sexual identity. I was being me as I understood myself. It was heaven. By twenty-four, I met Joel, who would become my longtime partner.

That summer after I moved in with Joel, my parents flew out to visit, obviously to assess what was going on. They were our guests, staying with us. Joel gave a party for them. He invited our friends and some of his colleagues at the time. They included celebrities and some really fab gay men of whom I have the fondest of memories. It was that kind of life. The life you think will last forever. My parents were dazzled.

Before the party, my dad pulled Joel aside. In the kitchen, Dad presented to Joel a bottle of single-malt scotch. He opened it and poured a glass for Joel. In a toast to my partner, Dad said, "I'm so glad that Michael has found a person like you." Isn't that the most beautiful thing?

My mother is a different story. The following year in late June, early Sunday morning, having returned from an all-night party at Probe, and on the eve of the LA Pride parade, my younger sister Nancy rang up. It was a polite conversation. I kept my conversation with Nancy brief. She handed the phone to my mother.

We had done LSD—Teddy Bears, or maybe it was Rainbow. Teddy Bears were gummies and Rainbow was a tiny piece of blotter paper. Before it was made illegal, LSD had been used in therapy. Emotions, particularly the repressed kind, are easily expressed. Without thinking but on instinct, my end of the conversation shifted to telling my mother that whatever the minimal grievance or resentment I may still have held, I forgave her . . . for the two and a half years that she was in the hospital sick with lupus.

She was touched and thanked me. Having now softened my mother, I dropped the bomb.

"Oh, and by the way, your son is gay."

"You know I still love you. You're still a member of this family. Nothing about that's going to change. Just don't tell your father," she said.

Ha! Ha! Dad had already acknowledged my relationship with Joel. He'd said he was *glad* that we were together. That's the way my family was. Mother never really accepted it. She was very religious. I think she desperately wanted me to have children. I'm glad that I didn't. She was a kind and sweet woman, like her dad's mother, Amelia.

My dad was odd. We fought a lot, too. Not over sexual identity or relationships. But over politics and that he played favorites . . .

His mother, Grandma, was the first of my family who said that I might be gay. She was a Christian Temperance Alf Landon Republican who busied herself keeping up appearances. She was relentless and someone to be reckoned with.

The summer of 1992, I went home for a reunion. I met with Grandma. She had sold her house and was in assisted living. Over lunch she told me a story about a boy she knew many years ago, who lived in a town nearby and realized that he was "different" from everybody else.

"What happened to him?" I asked, feigning politeness.

"He committed suicide." Grandma had fixed her eyes on me . . . a sign of trouble ahead.

After returning her fixated eyes with two of my own, my reply was perhaps a little too glib: "That's too bad. I guess today he would've moved to California."

"Oh, you boys!" she exclaimed, definitely exasperated with me.

Gays, Represent!

One of the most touching things about the Old Gays is that we have become "honorary grandpas" to some of our fans who aren't accepted in their own families. Even though so much has progressed since we were kids, we know so many LGBTQ+ people are still getting bullied. Sometimes even by their own families. We love being role models for the younger generation. Having someone to look up to or aspire to be helped us be our authentic selves. Here's who we looked up to when we were young gaybies:

MICK:
Martina Navratilova and Harvey Milk

I thought it cool when Martina came out *and* that her rival Chris Evert Lloyd supported her. They left their competition on the tennis court. I think that's a wonderful thing.

Harvey Milk ran a storefront on Castro Street. He ran for supervisor of the city and county of San Francisco. It was big when he was the first openly gay man elected to public office. Alongside Mayor George Moscone, Harvey was gunned down by fellow supervisor Dan White. I share a birthday with Harvey. He was ruthless and shrewd, charismatic, and erratic. Surely, he would've been elected mayor, and who knows how far his career would've taken him.

JESSAY:
Patti LaBelle

In my thirties, I saw her perform at a pediatric AIDS benefit concert at the Universal Amphitheatre in Los Angeles. I will never forget seeing her belting out "Lady Marmalade," kicking her heels off, and rolling on the floor. I said, "Now, that is what I want to do." I was raised to stand still, be blank-faced when singing. No emotion. From then on, I didn't exactly kick off my heels, but she taught me to emote. She was just wonderful. She gave me a different kind of freedom than I'd ever known.

ROBERT:
Frank Lloyd Wright

Since I was very young, back to preschool, I was always playing in the dirt and making structures and roads and cities. I learned what the word "architect" meant and the fact that there were people who actually created structures. From that point in time, I knew I wanted to be an architect when I grew up. Somehow, I learned about Frank Lloyd Wright and was absolutely fascinated by what he was doing. I started collecting books about him. I learned that Wright was born on June 8, which was my birthday. Learning that just made me have an even stronger connection to him. That's about the only thing I would read when I was real young. I'll never forget the day he died, in 1958. My mom came into my room and said in a very soft voice, "Bob, I've got some bad news for you. Frank Lloyd Wright died." I have a little library of books on Wright, and still to this day, I will pull a book and I'll sit down, and I'll look through it. Topography was very important to his design and that had a major impact and influence on the art I make. It's become the fundamental block to my art.

BILL:
Van Cliburn

I was tremendously impressed with the classical pianist Van Cliburn. The way he played, his style. He was from Texas, a looming giant, about six-foot-five, with flaming red hair. I guess I had a thing for gingers. I played the piano from age seven to twelve, so he was very influential during my prepubescence. I didn't know if he was gay or not, but I had a feeling deep down in my loins that he was on our team. Turns out my early gaydar detection system worked. He was gay and married a mortician named Thomas, who eventually sued him unsuccessfully for palimony after seventeen years together.

....

7

GAY
LIBERATION

The Good Ol'
Days for the
Gays

The Golden Age of Gaydom happened between the free love '60s up until the AIDS crisis began around 1980. For the OGs, it was our first inkling of liberation, and boy, did we take advantage of the release. We're talking two decades of total decadence. "In those days you'd walk into a bar, see someone you'd like, go up and talk to them, find out where you were sexually, then go off together," Bill recalls fondly. We were having so much fun, we didn't know the wild times were going to come to a crashing halt. If we had, we would have made sure to stop and smell the flowers and the Brut cologne. So here's our best advice for today's and future LGBTQ+ generations, who are currently living through the most progressive time in history to be queer: Please be present and appreciate the good moments because nothing lasts forever. Except herpes. Please be safe, too.

MICK: The era was freewheeling. Anything goes, lots of drugs. It took place within a naiveté that no longer exists. A lot of gay men had lived sheltered, closeted lives where they watched straight men and women play. The mainstream of society had not accepted us yet. Once free, we took our freedoms to the extreme. You know, it's understandable. The difference between youth and adulthood is that when you're young, you think you'll last forever. Adulthood is all about mortality. There was excess in San Francisco, Hollywood, New York City, Key West, Laguna, Fire Island, Amsterdam, Mykonos, Rio, Germany, and Thailand! It was more than hedonistic. I mean, the sexual acts that were being done: people were getting a little carried away. The parties! It was fantastically fun! You never knew who or what was stalking in the shadows.

I LEFT MY INHIBITIONS IN SAN FRANCISCO

BILL: I had kept myself kind of hidden in the gay scene in Southern California, so when I moved to Northern California, I'd never been happier in my life. No one was looking after what I was doing. I could be my own person. It opened up the whole world for me.

ROBERT: Oh, when I moved to San Francisco in 1980, it was mouth-dropping. Harvey Milk was gone, but I remember seeing other gay icons hanging out on Castro Street, including his replacement, Harry Britt, as well as entertainers like Sylvester and gay erotic filmmakers, including Peter Berlin, who would be seen daily leaning against a building displaying the famous bulge in his crotch.

There were so many places catering to gay people, and we were everywhere out and proud on the street. It was like, oh my God, this is an incredible playground. Gay heaven on earth! The camaraderie of the community was unifying, too. Everybody was friendly. It was idyllic. Not only was gay life out in the open, but the political clout of the gay community was growing. The elections of Harvey Milk and pro-gay mayor Dianne Feinstein made it feel like, hey, the gays really have authentic power. It made San Francisco the place I wanted to be.

BILL: In the '70s in San Francisco, everybody worked. Everybody had money. Everybody was happy. It was New Year's Eve every night. For eight years, I was footloose and fancy-free. I had boyfriends lining up. You could go to a bar like Sutter's Mill during the week, pick up a trick, and think just nothing of it. If my friends and I didn't pick up a trick by two a.m., we would go to one of five bathhouses in the city, come home, get a couple of hours' sleep, get up again, and go to Polk Street for brunch. San Francisco treated me very, very well.

ROBERT: Polk Street, dubbed "The Gayest Street in San Francisco," was the precursor to the Castro, one of the first queer areas in the city. There were probably ten gay bars on Polk, including a nice piano bar and a place you could play pinball, plus Welcome Home, a restaurant that everyone went to, which was inexpensive, but a great place to take a date. They hired the hottest waiters and I dated one for many years. When I first moved there, I lived on Sacramento Street, a short walk to Polk Street. One of my roommates, Tom, was a bartender at one of the bars, called the Pacific Exchange, on Fillmore Street. I'd go over there late at night and hang out and he'd introduce me to everybody and teach me how to make fancy mixed cocktails. Back then my drinks of choice were scotch and vodka. Not together, of course.

Polk Street did not have the same intensity as the bars in the Castro did. As Castro Street developed, it quickly overshadowed Polk

Street as the place every gay (and straight) person should go, especially on Halloween eve, when massive crowds would fill Castro and overflow onto nearby streets, including Market. They'd close off the streets; everyone paraded in costumes—mermen, Little Orphan Annie, Richard Nixon. I'll never forget when two straight ladies drove up and got caught with all these guys around them, and wanted to go the other way. So six strapping gay guys picked up their Mercedes-Benz 230 SL convertible and turned it around so they could get out of the scrum. It was the funniest thing I ever saw.

ROBERT: A couple friends once counted the gay bars in San Francisco, and they came up with two hundred or more.

BILL: The gay bars were all around the city—it wasn't just the Castro. Russian Hill, the Italian section of Grant Avenue, had two or three gay bars alone.

ROBERT: Picking up somebody was easy to do. It was a matter of trying out different places. I found my favorites. Midnight Sun was a music video bar. That's where I became familiar with entertainers like Cher, who was very active early in the video era. Midnight Sun was one of my favorites because it was a pickup bar on Castro, two blocks from Market. If you wanted to meet someone, it was almost guaranteed. It had gained a certain amount of notoriety beyond San Francisco. A lot of tourists and out-of-towners would go there, so you'd meet interesting people. One night, I was talking to this younger, very nice-looking, well-built man. After chatting with him for a while, I learned he was a dancer with the American Ballet Company, which was in town on tour. It was one of those rare, warm, beautiful San Francisco nights, so we drove out to Lands End Lookout, a very popular beach. We parked and ran down the steep hillside. We took off our clothes and climbed up on a big rock, and we had sex with the surf pounding around us. It was one of the most incredible sensual experiences I've ever had.

THE HEYDAY OF WEST HOLLYWOOD

BILL: In the '60s, West Hollywood was already known as a gathering place for gay men, but it was very low-key. I remember Rock Hudson had just done *Pillow Talk* with Doris Day, and the studios were going crazy trying to keep him off Santa Monica Boulevard because he would go into the bars there. I knew a guy who told me he and Rock met, but they were both tops. They saw this cute guy with a great ass across the room, and boom, they took him home. But Rock had to be really careful. He had to mind his p's and q's. In fact, we didn't even call him Rock when we were out. When we were in nice restaurants, we didn't want to gossip and get him in trouble. So we gave him a secret nickname; we called him "Stones."

Tab Hunter was not as flamboyant. Tab was different from most of his peers, because at thirty, he was older than everyone else. He hung out mostly in the Valley because he was a big equestrian. He loved horses.

Not a single bar from that era exists today. There was the Four Star in Beverly Hills, next to the Troubadour. That's where most of the Hollywood guys went. And the Red Raven, on the corner of Melrose and La Brea, right around the corner from Pink's hot dog stand. I was hanging out in WeHo from ages sixteen to twenty, so I needed a fake ID and was able to procure one at the Red Raven. A guy who just got out of the service said, "Hey, it's a shame you can't go in there. Here, try this." Boom, I got my fake ID. It was a nice bar, but it was swarming with undercover cops. In San Francisco, the cops had seen it all and left us alone. The LAPD were nasty to the gays. A nice guy I knew, a schoolteacher, he came into the Red Raven, saw a buddy of his, shook his hand, and was arrested.

MICK: In LA, you never knew if you were gonna hit on an undercover officer. I went to the leather bars, but I didn't have sex there because I didn't want to get arrested.

BILL: Down the street from the Red Raven was a beer bar called the Annex West. It wasn't for bikers necessarily, but it was for mainly the butch crowd. There was a group of guys that used to hang out at the Annex West, and they had pools. All I'd have to do is make a call on Saturday to find out where to be on Sunday. There was no dope, no drugs, but lots of drinking and barbecued steaks.

JESSAY: I would go to Rage and Mickey's, a little hole in the wall strip club. Thursday, Friday, and Saturday nights at Oil Can Harry's in Studio City. I got into country music because my partner and I wanted to dance together. It changed our lives. It was wonderful because I love holding and being held. Tuesday and Thursday they had line-dancing lessons. Friday night was gay night. Saturday night was disco night. Child, we were all in heaven. It was a hoot, and I miss it. Studio One had a disco and a cabaret, and that is where I did my first secular show. It was the first time I'd ever worked with a live band. I packed the house three times one weekend.

MICK: There was Oil Can Harry's on Ventura Boulevard in North Hollywood or Studio One in West Hollywood where we went out to dance. In Los Angeles on Highland Avenue at Waring, there was Probe. Probe was the big party place. The timeline went this way: Saturday night you'd gather at Greg's Blue Dot Bar. A block down from Probe on Highland, Greg's Blue Dot was where everybody went into the stalls and did cocaine. Just before midnight as you gathered outside of Probe you'd take a Teddy Bear or Rainbow. There was dancing and partying until morning. On Sunday at six a.m., Probe would close down, and Greg's Blue Dot would reopen. You'd then gather at Greg's for "church." There you'd order a bloody Mary, a vodka and orange juice, or a vitamin water. Anything to hydrate and ease yourself out of the inevitable crash.

In the 1980s, when visiting Manhattan in New York City, we'd stop at the Saint to dance. At the Saint I experienced MDMA for the first time, also known as E, ecstasy, or molly. We'd do the aerosol thing. You'd spray a little bit of inhalant into the corner of a handkerchief, fold it neatly, stick the rag's wetted corner into your mouth, breathe in, and then dance.

BILL: Everyone was doing drugs, all my peers were doing it, it was just a fact of life. You'd go to parties and people would come out of the bathroom and you'd say, "Hey, you got some white stuff on your nose." I knew a guy called Black Charlie. Charlie was six-foot-four, skinny as a rail, and dressed to the nines. He wore tailored double-breasted suits. He'd always come around with a paper bag filled with cocaine. He came to see us in our design showroom on Friday afternoons. In exchange for the cocaine, I'd give him clear plastic MDA gel tablets which gave you an absolutely wonderful high. Whereas acid would come and hit you right in the face, MDA would just take you up to new level after new level. MDA loosened any inhibitions I ever had. I became alive. After Black Charlie left, we'd go down to Sutter's Mill, and we'd drink until about nine o'clock. We'd go home, get changed, then go out again for the entire evening, either to the Castro or Polk Street. We did lots of drugs but we had rules, too. You could only take MDA on the weekends; otherwise it really interfered with work.

ROBERT: I went to Studio 54 in New York City. A who's who of celebrity showed up there: Andy Warhol, Brooke Shields, Cher, Salvador Dalí, Michael Jackson, Truman Capote. There would always be a line out front, and the doorman would govern who got in and who didn't. It was really hard to get into.

This was around 1978, when I had this large real estate business and had hired an attractive young ex-marine to work for us. In casual conversation, I learned that he had never been to New York City. So I booked us a hotel reservation at the ritzy St. Regis and plane tickets. Well, right after we arrived, he tried to find out ways he could pick up women. The first night, he rented a limo and went off by himself. So I went off by myself to barhop between some of the gay dives in the West Village and enjoyed myself. Nowadays, the area is super trendy and has been taken over by high-end hipster stores. Back then, my memory of Christopher Street was that it was very dark and dangerous. It was on the edge of the Village, near the Hudson River piers, so it was considered the low-rent district. I remember finding the Stonewall Inn, the epicenter of the gay revolution. But I was too intimidated to go inside!

The next day I asked him how his night was, and he said it wasn't great. He showed up to Studio 54 in a limo, but they wouldn't let him in. I was curious about Studio 54 and wanted to see what it was like, so we went back together the next night. We stood at the back of the line behind a sea of people, when all of a sudden, the doorman, who was sitting on a stool, pointed at me. "Who, me?" I mouthed, pointing at myself. "Yes," he mouthed back. We hadn't been there more than five minutes before we got in. We had a blast. I got drunk and danced on the stage with the marine. People in costumes wandered around the club. I remember sitting on a deep sofa, looking up drunkenly, and there was Raggedy Ann. I'll never get over the fact that the marine put on this big show of being Mr. Hot Stuff and couldn't get into Studio 54 and poor little ol' me got in immediately. I guess I looked like someone frequent patron Andy Warhol might find fascinating; I was very artsy-fartsy and extremely gay. I was also really tall and lean, and that usually helps me stick out in a crowd.

MICK: One of the best discos I ever went to was in Amsterdam in 1981. It was my first trip to Europe. It was the first place where I'd seen straight and gay people mixing together. There were a lot of young people hanging out, not drinking at all. I remember meeting a Dutch guy who was a speed skater. He was six-foot-two and blond, wearing white compression pants. He had the largest . . . *thighs* I'd ever seen. Sigh.

STEAMY NIGHTS
IN THE BATHHOUSES

In the '70s, gay men were offered fulfillment of their sexual fantasies at the bathhouses. Infamous in cities across the country and abroad, bathhouses ranged from the seedy to the spectacular. For a small guest fee, as low as $4, you could have sex with one or more men in rooms both public and private. Voyeurism, the art of watching, was encouraged. It was where partnered men met lovers, dates, and escorts for discreet prearranged sessions. Once let in through the locked doors, the scene and smell inside the bathhouses was ELECTRIC. Picture gaggles of towel-clad and/or naked men of all shapes, sizes, and diversity, wandering about in a blissful and mostly chemical-induced determination to worship the libido. Still, for the most part there was a "no drugs on the premises" policy that was enforced. Not forgotten was the distinct aroma of bleach mixed with sweat, semen, and amyl nitrite. This was a time for sex with no shame or apology.

Sex wasn't the only draw of the bathhouses; they were places to chill, network, and socialize freely. It was a line of communication, pre-Internet. They were also open on major holidays so that gay men estranged from their families had somewhere to go.

BILL: The bathhouses were so much fun. I'd go mainly on the weekends if I didn't pick up a trick. The biggest in town was Bob's, which was at the foot of Broadway, almost to the piers. There was one in the Tenderloin. Another one on Polk Street. But the biggest, my favorite, was called Ritch Street Health Club, south of Market in an alley. It was in a converted old brick building. In the basement they had lockers and a cafeteria that overlooked a giant stage. They had a hot tub on the stage, and behind the hot tub was the showers. So you could be sitting there having a sandwich watching guys play in the pool or jack off in the showers. Up on the third floor, in the middle of the room, was just one big orgy. There were at least fifty people there.

ROBERT: At the Ritch Street bath, the showers were strategically located within visual distance where you could sit and snack so you could watch people taking showers. There was another bath that was in the Tenderloin, called Mac's, and somehow they had gotten a Mack truck into the building, and you could play in the truck's cargo area and also the cab. Trucker fantasies.

MICK: The bathhouses in San Francisco were legendary. I used to go up there when I was dating Bob Landy. I went to my very first bathhouse in LA with a kid from Long Island named Chris Barone. We met that summer in Laguna. Chris took the role of a big brother. One day he said, "You're coming with me." I got in his VW van, and we drove to West Hollywood.

"What do I bring?" I asked innocently.

"Just yourself, and a cock ring. You can get everything else you need there," Chris answered.

The bathhouse was called 8709 because the address was 8709 West Third Street. You entered around the corner, from the alley. The bathhouse was across the street from Cedars-Sinai Hospital. If you blacked out or your dick fell off, they'd carry you over to the emergency room.

We drove up to West Hollywood, parking the van along the LA side of Burton Way. The next block over at the corner of George Burns and Third Street, across from Joe Allen, stood a building with no windows . . . the 8709.

There, among the white-towel-clad men, I met the crème of gay Los Angeles.

At a late 1970s–era bathhouse, the idea was to be a team-oriented, multipartnered slut. The layout of the 8709, as I remember, emphasized circulation, multi-ejaculation, and frequent orgasm. You get the idea? This is not the place for deep or frank conversation. You discuss top, bottom, or vers? Rubber or raw? Roleplay? Rough or vanilla?

I was introduced to slapping. I didn't like it, being that I was on the receiving end. Now, I'm into slapping my pecs, abs, buttocks . . . punching, too. Toughens the psyche. Stiffens resolve.

There were the showers, inviting open rooms for group action, and each with a theme. Last, there were the private rooms. Each no larger than a cubicle, with a twin-sized mattress placed on a platform constructed from plywood.

I was intimidated, this being my first visit. Mr. Wallflower stood in a hallway . . . watching the show. Just when I was really getting down on myself because I wasn't getting any . . . a man's man stood next to me. With bedroom, dark, longing eyes, I was seduced by Glen Dime.

Glen said he was working on his PhD in psychology (true). He was putting himself through his doctorate working in porn. He advertised in *Frontiers* . . . the yellow pages in the back. He had a lover. They shared an apartment in Hollywood. We found a cubicle.

Hours later, I'd realized that Chris and I were to rendezvous at a time that was long past. Knowing that I didn't know the fuck where I was, I began to panic. Glen was wonderful. He said I could go along with him and he'd drive me back to Laguna Beach. After I moved to Los Angeles, I saw Glen many times training at the Athletic Club on Santa Monica Boulevard in West Hollywood. By then he was in his residency and seeing a different type of client. Nice man. I miss Glen.

Meanwhile back at the 8709, I got dressed, left, and found the van still parked in its original spot. I knocked. A visibly cross Chris opened the van and let me in. He was sleeping. I joined him. That afternoon driving back on the freeway, my mentor said to me that he had worried . . . that I'd been "abducted." He'd gone cubicle to cubicle and knocked door to door looking for me. I'd felt a little responsible. At that time, I had no idea how I looked or behaved, or the effect my actions had on particular types of men. Later on I learned that the nickname that had been given to me was "Bambi."

DRAG SHOWS

JESSAY: My college roommate Glenn and I discovered that we were both gay, and we clicked. We never dated, but we used to put on drag shows in our dorm room. It was crazy how we got away with this at a church school in Chattanooga. We weren't allowed to do that secular stuff! A select few knew. Glenn would go out and round up the five guys we knew wouldn't tell on us. There was at least one straight guy. They'd sneak into our room and be the audience. We'd close the door, turn the lights down low, and perform. We wrapped our heads and bodies in towels, to mimic turbans and dresses, and dance and lip-sync to the Motown stars of the day, like the Supremes. We were very serious about it. There was no sex going on. I wished for it, but there wasn't. I was lusting after the guys who were there but played it off like it was all about the performance. We had to be kind of quiet because there were no locks on the door and the dean could walk in any second. I really don't know how we got away with our dorm room drag shows.

Somehow, we found out about this gay bar in town called the Cot. We were in a new dorm wing where all the windows opened. In the rest of the dorm, they didn't open. But lucky for us, ours did. Better yet, we were on the first floor. Saturday nights after room check, we'd climb out the window and go into town to the Cot. We'd meet other gay guys from college who would be scared and so they would dodge us. I'd tell them, "What, you think we're gonna go back and say we saw so-and-so at a gay bar?" Duh.

Anyway, the queen's name at the Cot was Candy Cane. She was this tall, older drag queen who didn't wear a wig. A woman that old and she's still kicking her legs that high? I was captivated. I loved going down there and knew I would love to do drag someday, but I didn't know how to do makeup. When I tried to do my face, I looked like a clown. It might be the only straight thing about me: I cannot do makeup.

CRUISING CULTURE

When George Michael was caught cruising in a public park in Beverly Hills, he famously told the photographer, "Are you gay? No? Then fuck off! This is my culture!"

Way before ANON hookups on Grindr, way before Casual Encounters on Craigslist, gay men had to work much harder to find each other. Cruising in not-so-secret public places has been an integral part of queer life dating back to the 1600s. The spoken word was unnecessary, and no commitment was needed.

Cruising is a skill that when practiced to perfection is elevated to art. The cruising artist relies on instinct. He is highly attuned to not-so-subtle signals—a furtive glance, the honed stare, grabbing on to oneself or the other guy by the crotch, standing next to a bush or urinal, taking one's dick out to piss, and so on. Finally, the artist must understand the signals. Like picking up on a hot-looking undercover cop ready to put the handcuffs on you for lewd conduct in public.

Queer identification is rooted in cruising. In Mick's eyes it was the homoerotic porn art of Touko Valio Laaksonen, aka Tom of Finland, that not only helped inspire him to come out but also served as de facto role models. "I wanted to be a Tom of Finland model," Mick says. "What I learned from his bio was that Touko himself was inspired by cruising. During his formative years living in World War II–era Helsinki, and at great risk, Touko sneaked to a nearby public park for sex. In defiance of the night curfew, Touko would watch or hook up with scores of cruising German Wehrmacht and SS officers."

Even with all the digital apps today, cruising thrives. There are corners of this country, and many countries around the world, where being out and proud is still very dangerous. Cruising may be the only option. For others, "sex hunting" is a thrill or kink, and the risk of getting caught in flagrante delicto in a bush or public toilet makes sex super-hot. "There's always been this fascination of, where do you go in the middle of the afternoon?" Bill says. "You've got the day off, where do you go to meet someone? Especially when the bars didn't open until five p.m."

All the Old Gays have done their fair share of cruising and lived to tell the torrid tales. "Cruising is pretty much everywhere," Mick says. "I've been picked up in department stores, the gas station, the mall, hardware stores, Circus of Books, the gym. When I moved to California and drove across the country, I picked up one guy at a casino in Reno, the next day a Continental Airlines steward, and subsequently the next day a beautiful Black man who was an opera singer. He was friends with Donna Summer. He told me she had a gorgeous German bodybuilder lover who left her. And when she became very famous, she turned to him and said, 'Payback's a bitch, baby.'"

GAY BEACHES

MICK: After moving to Southern California, my gay social life began at the beach. There are many gay beaches I've spread myself out on. Sitges in Spain, Ostia outside of Rome, Key West, South Laguna, which is where I met John Tristram. Brooks Avenue Beach in Venice, a short walk from two very serious gyms. And Will Rogers State Beach, below Pacific Palisades. When I became single again I'd visit Will Rogers by myself. Sometimes I'd meet up with a guy. We could walk off the beach, taking the tunnel underneath Pacific Coast Highway. The tunnel took you to Channel Road. A short walk up from there is a place called the Golden Bull. There you can enjoy early happy hour cocktails and a postbeach dinner. Fond memories there.

BILL: The Laguna Beach city fathers absolutely despised the fact that when tourists went to the main beach downtown, they were in such close proximity to a bunch of hot, Speedo-clad gays looking to hook up. The Hotel Laguna was a tourist spot, and right next to it was a gay beach anchored by two gay bars, Dantes and Barefoot. So the city remodeled the whole boardwalk, tore down the bars, and landscaped over it. Not to be deterred, we just moved down a little farther south.

PUBLIC TOILETS

MICK: The Union 76 on Melrose Avenue at the Hollywood Freeway was very popular when Scotty Bowers owned the station in the '60s and '70s. The Scotty Bowers I knew was a jack of many trades: bartender, escort, and gardener specializing in tree removal. You had to know where the play space that Scotty maintained was located. You had to have his permission to enter onto his property. It was populated with the hottest kind of trade looking for a blow job. Porn stars, LAPD and sheriff's officers on break, and the California Highway Patrol.

Scotty was cool, and he liked me. I smile when I remember how we met. My partner Joel had taken me to a holiday party at a house high above Hollywood, which overlooked the Hollywood Bowl. Inside Scotty was bartending. Joel introduced me to Scotty, who smiled at me big, with eyes all lit up. Joel asked him politely, "Scotty, can you stir Michael's drink special-like?" Scotty took me behind the bar with my drink in hand. Without hesitation he undid his fly, pulled out one of the most battered, cut, BIG cocks I'd seen so far, and shoved it into my Manhattan over ice, stirring counterclockwise. When we returned, Joel admonished me to close my jaw, which had been implanted on the floor.

PARKS

ROBERT: The first time I cruised a park was in college in St. Louis. It was by an old Civil War cannon in Confederate Circle. I recall driving by there, and I'd see cars parked along this little lane. One day I decided to see for myself. I drove around and looked into the windows of the cars and saw guys sitting alone in them. They would look very intently at passersby, and every once in a while, one of them would make a gesture, like, *Come here.* Or nod their head.

The first time that I made contact with somebody, we drove off together and went to where this person lived. That was probably my first real total sexual experience. I was around eighteen years old. I never recalled feeling traumatized in any way by it. It was mainly a feeling of, *Okay, I've satisfied my curiosity about this. I now know what's going on.* After processing it for a little bit, I went back and went a little deeper into the subculture, if you will.

When I first moved to San Francisco, I lived with a couple of guys I already knew in a small apartment on Sacramento Street. After a few months we decided we liked each other well enough to live together, but we needed a much larger living space. We found a great ground-floor apartment not far from the Castro, a couple blocks below Buena Vista Park. I had brought my dog from St. Louis, JT, a German shepherd, and I would walk him every day up the steep hill to Buena Vista Park. I found out quickly there was cruising going on in that park twenty-four hours a day. I met some really interesting people there and observed some steamy sexual activity going on in the rustling bushes. Pretty soon I was shaking the sugar trees myself with various men. One time, during the day, I was walking on one of the back paths, and I came upon the most beautiful blond guy sunning naked on a blanket. I was kind of taken aback. "Oh, hi, who are you?" I said. He ended up coming back to my house with me and we had sex. I would reencounter him a number of times afterward.

I learned that he was a porn star and his screen name was Mark. One of our encounters is particularly memorable. It was a day when I had been invited down to a friend's house in Hillsboro for an evening dinner to meet some of his friends. Mark dropped by my house that morning and greeted me with "Hi, it's a beautiful day! Let's drop some acid and go to Lands End Beach for a while and play." Not thinking of the consequences, I agreed, and after somehow making our way to the beach, we spent the next several hours running through the fields and woods adjacent to the beach and along the beach with reckless and gay abandon, which was one of the most mind-blowing events of my life. Somehow, I managed to collect my wits enough to realize I needed to get back home and get ready for my dinner party in Hillsboro, which was a forty-five-minute drive.

Not being a frequent user of acid, I didn't realize that it has rather long-lasting effects and it suppresses one's appetite. Again, miraculously I managed to get ready and drive the distance and made it to my friend's house in time for the party. My friend greeted me and ushered me into the house and introduced me to his friends, which included the daughter of the CEO of one of San Francisco's largest banks, a vice president of Pepsi, and several other notable people from the Bay Area.

And there I was, about to engage in meaningful conversations and share a wonderful meal with these newfound friends, the only problem being I had fireworks going off in my vision and no desire to eat at all. Somehow I made it through the evening, up to and including being seated at the dinner table, but when I started passing on courses or taking very small portions, my friend finally asked me if anything was wrong. Was I not hungry?

I asked him if I could talk to him in the kitchen. When we were alone, I explained the whole day's events. He burst out laughing and almost fell to the floor. After he recovered, he ushered me back into the dining room and proceeded to tell everyone seated at the table what I had just told him. Everybody had a good laugh, and I ended up having one of the best days of my life. No judgment from anywhere or anybody. Just living life to its fullest. I realized then I'd definitely made the right decision to move to California.

MICK: In Hollywood, there's a place called Wattles Mansion between La Brea and Fairfax that has beautiful gardens and trails. I went there to cruise sometimes when I had free time.

JESSAY: Everybody in LA went to Griffith Park. I used to go by myself after my partner Don died. There was a spot there where I'd lie out with my umbrella and watch all the hot guys worship the sun. The most popular cruising spot was parking over by the zoo and the train station. Gosh, that was amazing. I'd never get out of my car until somebody came to me. I am not the aggressor, but once I've connected, I get a little braver. It's my insecurity still to this day. I'd wonder, "Am I cute enough? Am I worthy of this? Am I good-looking? Do people like me?" I'd sit in my Chrysler until I got the look from someone, then go up in the woods, and wham, bam, thank you, ma'am. Sometimes there would be repeats. I was more of a repeat person. I feel like I'm the only person who falls in love with someone they met cruising. That's why I'm careful with what I do. My heart is tender. I love love. And I can fall too easily, so I tried to protect myself from being used just for sex. I wanted more than that. But it was very exciting. Like, what's going to happen sitting in that car? Is somebody going to look at you from their car and approach? It was fun and it was validation that you look good. 'Cause I had some handsome men. I wasn't out there all the time, but when I got a chance, it was just a thrill. The thrill of the hunt!

BILL: Griffith Park was a hot place for cruising. It was notoriously dangerous because plainclothes LAPD would go up there to trap gays. I went once, but I thought, *This isn't right for me. I want to be happy making connections, not terrified.* A lot of the same guys who went to Griffith Park did the restroom scene, too. That was just way too public for me, and it all scared the life out of me.

MICK: I wasn't lucky in Griffith Park. I did try on occasion. What I remember is a lot of overgrown brush and vegetation. Literally a canopy, all of which was hidden. There were many people who had sheltered there, went there to shoot up, and there was a ton of waste, including used needles. That, plus my fear of coyotes and rattlesnakes—it wasn't the place for me.

LIFESTYLES OF THE GAY AND FAMOUS

Back in the day, we had some run-ins with a few living legends. Life was such a gas!

MICK: By chance, I met Rock Hudson in Laguna Beach at the Boom Boom Room. It was winter 1979. I'd driven back from a rehearsal at UC Irvine. Not ready to drive up Aliso Canyon Road and back to the house, I parked in front along Pacific Coast Highway. What I recall is that we were the only two people in the front bar. He was a nice, personable man who was a MOVIE STAR. We had a conversation . . . small talk I don't remember. As it turns out, Rock was friends with a guy I'd later meet. He became a strong influence in my life, Bart Turner.

In Hollywood, we were social with actors, writers, and directors. We'd attend parties where it was always a mixed crowd. That's where I met people who worked in the industry. Often these events included games like charades. That's how I met Markie Post, of *Night Court* fame, and Albert Hague, the professor on the TV series *Fame*. Frequently the parties were held at the house of a manager we were close with, Bob Manahan, and his lover Chuck. When *Time* magazine published the first ten thousand people who died from AIDS, Bob and Chuck were among them.

BILL: When I was underage, I couldn't go to bars, but I could go to coffeehouses, like 8727 Melrose, which was across the street from the Pacific Design Center. One day, a white-haired gentleman came up to me and said, "Excuse me, you don't know me, my name is Jimmy Pendleton. I'm having a party, and I'd like to know if you would like to attend."

"Can I have a couple minutes to think about this?"

"Certainly." We really did talk like the old movies back then.

I asked my friends about him, and they said, "Oh, that's Jimmy Pendleton! You should go!" Jimmy was an interior designer and a very clever man. He could dance, he had a wit about him, and when he told stories he would have everyone in stitches the entire time. In Miami he met an heiress, Mary Francis, whose nickname was Dodo. Dodo wasn't a great beauty and she had a clubfoot, but Jimmy adored her. There was no doubt that Jimmy was gay, and even though she was his beard, he always had Thursday nights out. It was an arrangement that he had with Dodo.

Jimmy's house was built on the flat streets right next to the Beverly Hills Hotel, right before you go up into the hills. Prime real estate. Jimmy hired the same architect who built Lucille Ball's house, a very handsome man by the name of John Elgin Woolf, and the house was constructed in 1942. When asked about the style of the house, Jimmy coined the phrase "Hollywood Regency." It was absolutely the most spectacularly elegant home I'd ever seen in my life. You'd drive through a large hedge into a gravel driveway. When I knocked on the door, Phillip, the butler, opened the door and greeted me. Phillip was a mature man. Gray hair, white coat with four buttons and white shirt, black tie. As gracious as could be.

The house was pure opulence. The vestibule floor was white marble parquet and featured a marble column with an armless bust of a young man. Phillip led me down the hallway, opened a set of double doors, and before me was a sea of the most gorgeous men I'd ever laid eyes upon. Everyone was in coat and tie. I was dressed to the nines as well. I wore my traditional navy-blue blazer, gray slacks, white button-down shirt, and striped tie. Almost all the guys were dressed the same way. At the other side of the room there was a fireplace flanked by two humongous windows that overlooked the pool, pool house, and rose garden. Way at the back of the property was a eucalyptus grove.

I found out later that the party I attended was the first gay party that Jimmy had after Dodo died. He was fully out by then and ran an antique store on the Sunset Strip. Luckily, my parents had weaned me on fine dining, so I knew which fork and knife to pick up at the right time.

Jimmy gave me a personal tour of his house, which he christened "Woodland." (In the '60s, legendary producer Robert Evans bought the house. It became the site of some of the biggest movie deals in Hollywood history, and appeared in the documentary *The Kid Stays in the Picture*. It's now an historic property in Beverly Hills, and the current owner is David Zaslav, CEO of Warner Bros. Discovery.) The first thing Jimmy showed me was this beautiful Modigliani painting. He also had Picassos. This was art I'd only seen in books, never in person. The home was a classical masterpiece, impeccably decorated to the hilt with only the finest furniture and china. After my private tour, one of his friends said, "Hey, Bill, come here, I wanna show you something." We walked into Jimmy's room, and there were buzzers on either side of the bed. "This one will call Phillip to bring him his warm milk. This one, he'll give Jimmy a blow job."

Jimmy turned out to be the kindest man. His parties weren't hookup orgies; rather, they were elegant affairs attended by a lot of well-connected gay couples. I was one of the few singles invited. I made two or three tricks out of the gatherings, but it was more about networking. I met enough people at Jimmy's parties who helped to launch me into Hollywood–Beverly Hills gay society. Like Herbert Hirschmiller, a spice broker for the Spice Islands. Bruce Nelson, one of the biggest real estate brokers in Hollywood. And there was a gorgeous young guy who claimed to be an heir to the Coca-Cola fortune and who was a clothing designer. He was from Atlanta and affected an English accent.

Here's one of my favorite stories from that time: When I was modeling, I posed for Jack Hyde, the West Coast editor of *Menswear* magazine. Jack was different from a lot of the fashion people of that time. He went into the navy out of high school, graduated from college, went to work in journalism, and ended up working for Fairchild Publications, which owned *Menswear*, *W*, and *WWD*.

Jack literally lived on Melrose Place. It was only two blocks long but centrally located at the corner of Melrose and La Brea. He had a party, and I met Iris Bauer, the fashion editor of *Look* magazine. Iris and her assistant Tom had come out to the West Coast to see what the scene was like. It was her first visit to Southern California. I had just bought myself a five-year-old Mercedes-Benz 190 SL hardtop convertible. I told Iris, "I'd be happy to drive you around and show you Hollywood and Malibu." And she said, "Can Tom come?" and I said, "Sure!" Even though it was a two-seater. Tom had to squeeze into the back.

So I took them all around Hollywood, we ladies-who-lunched in Malibu, then I dropped them off at the Beverly Hills Hotel. "You've been so kind," Iris said, "Why don't you join Tom and me at the pool tomorrow?" I drove in the next day, valeted my Mercedes, then Tom took me up to his room to change, like I was Beyoncé at the Grammys. I had my driving clothes, then I brought separate pool attire. In those days you didn't walk through the lobby of the Beverly Hills Hotel in swim trunks. We went back down to the pool, where Iris bumped into her old friend Johnny Carson, who was lunching with Phyllis Diller. Johnny gave Iris a hug and asked, "Would you like to join us for lunch?" Then he looked at Phyllis and said, "Is Fang going to join us for lunch?" Fang was Diller's pet name for her husband. "No, he's too busy in the pool!"

I proceeded to have the most marvelous lunch, sipping iced tea and listening to Johnny and Phyllis banter back and forth. I didn't get a word in edgewise, and I didn't try. Johnny was so laid-back and friendly. I think he enjoyed showing off for me. Phyllis was over the top and "on" the entire time. They both were so charming and witty. It was one of the highlights of my youth. I got a ton of mileage out of that story for years, plus I didn't have to pay for lunch.

I met so many accomplished people working in the design showroom in San Francisco also. Zubin Mehta, the principal conductor of the LA Philharmonic in the '60s, opera tenor Sergio Franchi, ice skater Peggy Fleming, and Kathryn Crosby, Bing's bubbly wife, who would stop by after taking acting classes at the American Conservatory Theater. She had this effervescent personality. She would flit around the room, touching everything and giggling. She spent so much time with us, probably because Bing was always playing golf. Stevie Wonder's wife once came in during Market Week, and we had just gotten a new line of cordless lights for a piano. I was so oblivious and asked innocently, "Do you have a piano? This little light here really would help." She and her decorator both laughed. Later, the decorator came back and told me who she was.

Perhaps my favorite celebrity encounter was with a socialite by the name of Mrs. Rudolph A. Light, the silent-film star and ex-wife of J. Paul Getty, who she met when she was fourteen and got romantically involved with at twenty-one. She was absolutely gorgeous and she had been married five times. She was kicked out of Miami society because she was always inebriated, so she moved to San Francisco. She came into our showroom with a designer and announced she had just bought a penthouse on top of Nob Hill. She told us that she had an opium bed but, alas, she didn't have an opium pipe. Would we perchance have any resources where we could procure one? Well, we shot a wire off to our broker in England, stat, and they presented us with four or five choices. The one that we selected for her was bronze and had crustaceans walking all over the pipe.

I would go up to her apartment on Nob Hill, and she'd invite me up to show me what she'd done with the place. She'd announce, "Bill, I have to get ready for a dinner party," then get dressed, with a vodka in one hand and a cigarette in the other. I watched her walk down the hall, literally bouncing off her collection of Picasso paintings.

San Francisco had a very big social hierarchy. She was running with the A group, so she tried to be good. But she always showed up late to everything, usually drunk, occasionally almost passing out in her soup. So she eventually was exiled from the San Francisco socialite crowd, too, and highballed and hightailed it back to Miami. She'd come to make a new beginning. But the new beginning was like her old ending. She may have worn out her welcome in every city in America but never with me. I miss her to this day.

Las Vegas real estate tycoon and art collector Steve Wynn would board his Circus Circus private jet and fly to San Francisco's private airport, Butler Aviation. I would leave the showroom to pick up Steve and his wife and take them to our showroom. When they were finished, if they weren't staying overnight, I would drive them back to Butler Aviation and they'd take off in the big clown jet back to Vegas.

We had several designers from Las Vegas who loved our showrooms and one of their clients was Liberace. Liberace had a home on a corner lot in Las Vegas. It was a tract home that he did up in his own style. Then he bought the home behind it and connected the two. He built a forty-foot-long atrium that had four recesses in the ceiling, and over each recess was a chandelier. Under each chandelier was a three-tiered limestone fountain. The floors were all travertine; the walls were all mirrored. He used the back house for his personal life. He had a boyfriend at that time who lived with him. His bedroom was vast, and in one corner was this huge round bed. Above it, he had commissioned an artist to paint Michelangelo's *Creation of Adam* from the Sistine Chapel. On the ceiling of his boyfriend's room, there was a painting of Liberace himself in black tie, conducting, surrounded by all these little Italian angels playing different instruments.

Our designers would invite us down to his house when he was doing a new show with the ballet company at one of the colleges in Nevada. After the show, he invited all his friends to his house. They picked us up in two Rolls-Royces: The first one was a Phantom, and that's what we rode in. And the luggage was carried in the other, a Corniche convertible. And up and away we went. We spent a week down there having the most surreal time of our lives.

Liberace could charm the pants off you. He didn't get into my pants, though. He had a partner at the time . . . not sure that made a difference. He was so nice to me. There really wasn't any secrecy around his being gay at this point. This was past the time when he won the lawsuit against *Confidential* magazine. So even though everybody knew, the fact that he won the case just shut it down. The ladies always loved Liberace anyway. In fact, at his show, he walked down to the front row and there was this little blue-haired lady. He put out his hand and said, "Do you like my ring?"

"Oh, Liberace, it's so beautiful," she purred.

"Thank you; you helped buy it."

Homophobia Never Held Us Back

Did you know that 33 percent of LGBTQ+ people have experienced discrimination in the last year? That goes up to 60 percent for transgender peeps. And nearly 46 percent of us are still in the closet at our jobs because we fear the repercussions of being out. All the Old Gays have experienced homophobia in their lives. Mmm, Bill not so much, because he was insulated in the uber-swishy design world most of his career, and he believes this fabulously faggoty fortress shielded him from homophobia. Other than during his early Speedo days in Laguna Beach, he can't recall experiencing overt discrimination. On the other hand, Robert, Mick, and Jessay have powerful stories to tell about the discrimination they've faced in their lives and careers and how they figured out the best way to deal with it. Basically, Robert moved, Jessay prayed, and Mick said, "Screw it," and took control of his own fate.

Robert was run out of town

In 1978, my real estate empire was booming, but my relationship with my boyfriend Chris was imploding. The other battle I was waging at the time was with the establishment in St. Louis. It all came to a head when a pair of fifteen-story high-rise apartment buildings came on the market. They were kitty-corner from one another and both were heavily occupied by gay people who lived in the Central West End neighborhood. My partners, Roger and Mike, and I decided we wanted to buy those buildings. We were in the process of negotiating the contract when another developer came in underneath us and basically stole the two buildings from our grasp. After he bought the buildings, he instructed the building managers to start getting rid of the gay tenants to phase them out and replace them with straight people. The whole point was to get rid of the gays.

When I learned about that, it really pissed me off. We had just bought a seven-story apartment building called the Olympia, right next to the St. Louis University campus. So I started running ads in the local Central West End newspaper that said, "Responsible tenants welcome, regardless of race, religious beliefs, or sexual orientation." The response was overwhelming, because it was next door to the school, which was a Jesuit university.

At the time I was working at a nonprofit corporation founded by me in conjunction with St. Louis University called Newtown St. Louis. The goal was to revitalize an area known as Central City and bring in developers. The chairman of the board of the nonprofit was Paul Reinert, who was chancellor of St. Louis University and a Jesuit. He asked me to attend a meeting of the Jesuit community. I didn't know what the agenda was, but I went to the meeting anyway and found myself in a room chock-full of Jesuit priests. They started going through their agenda, when they got to an item about what to do about the homosexual issue in the Olympia apartments. It was a discussion about what actions they could take in order to make sure that the Olympia didn't become a hangout for homosexuals. Here I was, working for the university, drawing a paycheck. They knew of my involvement in real estate because I was very open with the board about whether or not they viewed my buying real estate in the area as a conflict of interest. In the past, they took the position that what I was doing was part of bettering the neighborhood.

I was not open about my homosexuality with the Jesuit board.

But I didn't hide myself either. So they kind of knew. But no one said anything, as long as I didn't do anything that would threaten them. They hadn't had any problem with me before, but now I had become a problem.

The Jesuit community came down hard on me about the Olympia apartments. Then the alderman of the ward called me and tried to guilt me into changing my advertising tactics. At a fundraising meeting for one of the candidates for governor of Missouri, banker John Obermann approached me with a clear threat. He was president of Commerce Bank, our biggest lender, which held many of the notes on our buildings. Obermann told me, "You need to know that there are a lot of people in this community concerned about your policies. It would be wise for you to give some thought to changing your policies. After all, we'd hate to see you lose everything you've built up at this point."

The message was clear. If I didn't toe the line, they were going to start pulling notes and basically steal the property my partners and I worked so hard to acquire and maintain. I ended up resigning my position with Newtown instead of folding to their demands.

A month later, I happened to attend a meeting of the National Trust for Historic Preservation being held at the Fairmont Hotel in San Francisco. I was in a bad place. I was at war with Chris. He was jealous of my real estate empire and how much time I spent working, and to strike back at me he started going out with other guys and flaunting it in front of my face to psychologically demean me. We were having heated arguments. I'd just had my entire livelihood threatened to be taken away. I climbed up a cropping near Buena Vista Park, and I sat on a rock for several hours looking out over the city, ruminating about my situation. I was so struck by the beauty and the freedom of San Francisco. In that moment, I had an epiphany—it wasn't worth it. I walked down the hill to a phone booth at the corner of Market and Castro, called my business partner Roger, and declared, "I'm moving to San Francisco."

Jessay reconciled the
relationship between God and the gays

Though all of us grew up in religious households—Robert was Southern Baptist, Mick Lutheran, and Bill Methodist—I'm the only one who has put faith front and center my entire life. I was born into the African Methodist Episcopal Church, and my mom, my sister, and I became Seventh-day Adventists when I was seven. I don't consider myself a religious person, but I am a spiritual person. We were in church Saturday and Sunday because it was a social outlet to me. I was a kid, and I just wanted to see my friends. Growing up with it, I heard what I heard, but I kept what I needed and let the rest go. Which was a lot of it. I just ignored all the hellfire and brimstone.

I try to be the kind of Christian that I think Christ would really be. I tell people that because there are times I don't agree with what's going on in the community. I don't know how I've gotten as far as I have being in the church. There are so many people who were hurt and kicked out. I don't know if it's my resilience or my "I don't give AF" attitude. A lot of gay folks leave the church, and I think that's sad, but understandable. It's hard for LGBTQ+ people to embrace organized religion when it's so often homophobic. There are some evil people who pretend to be religious. I'm scared of brand-new Christians. They scare the dickens out of me.

But I'm here to tell you, if you love the Lord and want to live a life of faith, there are more options than ever today that are LGBTQ+-friendly. You can find a church where you feel at home, a social environment that lifts you up. In my church, if there's something I don't like, I just let it go. For me, it's mostly about the music and the stories. I pick songs to sing that Jessay needs to hear.

There are days when I have my doubts about religion. But most of the time I don't nurse those doubts, because no matter what I go through or what I have been through, I have felt God's arms wrapped around me constantly, especially at low times. I've been a member of several congregations throughout my life but feel so blessed that

I found Glendale City Church in Glendale, California. I was in a drag show (I finally learned how to put on my face!) channeling Patti LaBelle, and a pastor came up to me and said, "You need to come to my church next week in drag." And I said, "Are you kidding? Do you know how much work this takes? No way." I showed up in my regular clothes and the female saxophone player in the church band was wearing the exact same dress I had worn when the pastor met me! It was fate. I've been going there ever since.

At Glendale City Church there is actual joy. I started singing at the Presbyterian church when I was sixteen, but I was bored. There's nothing worse than a minister who gets up there and talks with no energy. If you're not excited about your own stories, that'll put everyone to sleep. Besides, I'm about the music. If the music is crappy, it's hard to get me there. I ain't gonna lie, I need to be entertained, even in church. You need to hold my attention. I would love to go to a Black church, but I don't, because first thing they ask, "Are you married?" And I'm like, "Ain't none of your business, girl. Leave me alone." I quite miss my people, but I don't miss that part of it.

Glendale City Church is known as the worldwide gay church or the pink church. We have gay members from around the world. Luckily, at my church we have everything, even Black gospel. I love going up to people who are visiting our church and saying hi, because I know what it's like to walk into a church and nobody says anything. My church is a very welcoming place, and it's saved my sanity so many times. Here's what I love most about it:

The Community
It's a social thing for me. I look forward to getting ten million hugs every week. I have a wonderful circle of friends at my church, and we do a lot of community and charity work. I love Pride Month; it's a big thing at our church. It's gayness 24/7 for the entire month of June. And February is Black History Month. All our music is Black music for twenty-eight days, even though we're a (mostly) white choir.

The Words of Wisdom

My mom always told me to take what resonates and leave the rest, so that's what I've always done. I don't like ministers just doing the whole sermon on the worst part of the Bible. Give me some joy. As long as I'm hearing encouragement, I'll listen. My favorite passage is Psalm 23 because He's holding me together in my weakest moments.

> *The Lord is my shepherd; I shall not want.*
> *He maketh me to lie down in green pastures: he leadeth me*
> *   beside the still waters.*
> *He restoreth my soul: he leadeth me in the paths of*
> *   righteousness for his name's sake.*
> *Yea, though I walk through the valley of the shadow of death,*
> *   I will fear no evil: for thou art with me; thy rod and thy staff*
> *   they comfort me.*
> *Thou preparest a table before me in the presence of mine*
> *   enemies: thou anointest my head with oil; my cup runneth*
> *   over.*
> *Surely goodness and mercy shall follow me all the days of my*
> *   life: and I will dwell in the house of the Lord for ever.*

The Church Clothes

Honey, I like getting dressed up when I go out, period. I love clothes. They're a little tighter lately, but I still love them. The only things I will not wear to church are jeans and tennis shoes. I wear slacks and a nice shirt that I don't often get to wear during the week. I respect it that much. When I sing at weddings, sometimes I'm the most dressed-up one there. I was embarrassed about it at first. But my philosophy is, "I wanna keep going up, not down."

The Holidays

Easter is my favorite. Powers! Resurrection! Christmas is hard because it's just a tender little baby. And I like big! Send the sparks up behind my head. I just love the whole big production. Easter is when Christ died and rose again. That's why we've got the strength that we have because He did rise again. I think . . . I wasn't there, you know. But what I take it to mean is that resurrection is possible for all of us. It's the power to heal, to be restored. That's what the mystery of Easter means to me. And I love the pomp of it all.

Mick refused to be closeted in Hollywood

At twenty-four years old, I didn't question my sexual identity. I was just being me, you know? What I found appalling was the discrimination that I faced *after* coming out. It's amazing how people see you differently and, I believe, wrongfully judge you.

I was surrounded by homophobia at every turn. There's a lot of homophobia in the world of bodybuilding. Bob Paris was the top bodybuilder for, like, four years in a row? After he retired and came out, his name was obliterated from all the record books. Like he'd never existed. Considering that he was a star for so long and that he elevated the sport to a new level, the way they treated him was wrong.

The prejudice that I experienced? It got mixed up and confused with whether anyone was even going to hire me. I moved to California to become an actor . . . get my SAG card to work. I studied HARD, earning an MFA from UC Irvine. I was pretty darn good.

It's the 1 percent that we call "luck" that determined if I got work. And it mattered NOTHING if I was out or not. I did come to understand that it could mean the death of your career. Rupert Everett recalled in his autobiography being denied a role in a Sharon Stone film because he was gay, even though Sharon Stone wanted him for the part. A film executive called Rupert a "pervert" and claimed that half the movie theater owners in America were right-wing Christians.

I thought, *Well, if Rupert Everett can never get work, how could I?*

It's different today. Look at the career of Neil Patrick Harris and the trajectory it's taken.

The one agent I did manage to hire ended up firing me. It wasn't even that I was gay, it was that I was out. Yes. He asked me point-blank, "Are you gay?"

"Well, yes," I replied.

"Are you open about it?"

"I'm pretty open about it. I have a lover."

"Well, I'm not going to represent you anymore."

There were so many gay men I knew who were pretending not to be out so they could work in Hollywood, and it did cause tension in the community. I'm not going to mention names or things that I know. But I don't know how they can live with themselves. They may have justified it because their career came first. That's one of the changes I see, today. People are looking for authenticity. They can smell a fake a mile away, and they're not interested.

I chose to be authentic and was punished for it. Luckily, I got an MBA at Pepperdine, and that allowed me to have a backup plan. When I couldn't get acting work, I decided to set up my own business as a grant writer for nonprofits. Creating my own business and working for myself provided me with an income lasting twenty-five consecutive years.

A cool gig that I did for many years was stand-in work. Ray Clauson, an Emmy Award–winning set designer, got me my first stand-in job on the Academy Awards. Stand-in work is as described. You are hired to "stand in" for a presenter during rehearsals so that camera persons, lighting, and directors can set up and practice the shots that we see on the live broadcast. I was liked so much that I worked the entire award season show circuit—People's Choice Awards, American Music Awards, the Golden Globes, the Emmys, and the Grammys. It was enough money to pay my health insurance.

One time, I was working the American Music Awards and my call time at the Shrine Auditorium was for seven a.m. They asked us to sit in the audience, when suddenly, the curtain went up, and there stood none other than Diana Ross! We had our own private performance. Terrific! What a magnetic presence! I had never seen Diana Ross onstage before. Electric!

Yes, homophobia sucks, but I look at it as a glass half full. It forced me to pivot into a career that actually made me money. I was handsomely rewarded with celebrity encounters that I can tell all about at dinner parties and . . . in a book. In life, things happen for a reason. As they say, live in the moment, be patient, and trust the universe.

8

SEX

Bulges and Booties and Cuties, Oh My!

Things are gonna get a little spicy here, cha cha cha! Mmm-hmm, we love to talk about getting lucky. We don't think there's anyone else who worships crotches and asses as much as Robert does. Jessay may be a spiritual man, but he's a very sexual being, too. "I tell people, if it doesn't say '. . . and God said,' then I'm okay with it. God never said anything about homosexuality." Mick self-identifies as bi and is super sex-focused. He injects the subject into any conversation, much to the shyness/embarrassment of Bill, who calls himself "passionate vanilla" in the bedroom. Here's the thing. The four of us love lovin', but we are very different when it comes to matters of the heart and other body parts. Contrary to what many may think, gays are as diverse in their predilections as anyone else. We're not all into kinky boots and cock rings. Some of us are cuddle bunnies who love to spoon. Sometimes both are true.

So, okay, let's get into the fun stuff. Here's a candid conversation about all things sex, no filters, no holds barred. We left no stone unturned. "Stone" is not a euphemism for anything. Get your mind out of the gutter . . . Here we go!

WHAT'S YOUR TYPE?

MICK: Short, tall, and in between, they gotta have a great body . . . muscle attracts muscle.

JESSAY: You know what, I have always wanted to have sex with a Latino. I never have, but I think they are so sensual. I get that it's completely objectifying to say so, but hey, fantasy is all about it. I think Latinos look like good kissers, good cocksuckers, good rimmers. They just got it. There's always hope!

ROBERT: Toned. The whole package. Just a nice, toned body.

BILL: My favorite type is a lean, well-defined body. I guess I don't really have a type. A lot of people do, but to me it just depends on the individual.

WHAT'S YOUR IDEAL ROMANTIC DATE?

MICK: Dinner, red wine, dessert, and then a visit to his dungeon.

JESSAY: I'm a verbal person. I like to get to know you. I look into your soul while I'm looking at you. So, dinner, conversation, then sex.

BILL: Lying on the beach all day, taking a shower, having sex, then going down for an absolutely beautiful dinner. It ends up with us in each other's arms falling asleep in bed.

ROBERT: I was romanced by a guy in San Francisco, which I really enjoyed. He sent me flowers periodically right after we met. I would pick him up and when we'd drive around, and he'd put his hand on my leg. And that went on for a few weeks before we first had sex. The anticipation was hot.

DO YOU THINK WAITING TO HAVE SEX IS NECESSARY?

ROBERT: If I meet someone who I am really attracted to, I want to get to the sex quickly.

JESSAY: I don't plan it. I just get there and see what's gonna happen.

BILL: I'd sleep with 'em right off the bat. I think sex is a very important part of any relationship, and I think you should know what you're getting into, because yes, you can fall in love with a person, but what if they're lousy at sex? Then what? I'd rather get that out of the way first and set boundaries later.

MICK: As far as the dungeon is concerned, my OGs don't know what they're missing. Still, one always dives headfirst into a lit pool with eyes open. The protocol that I follow begins with me: the bottom interviews the top first. Then the top interviews me. Through the process of discovery, the two of us close in on where there is "trust" and what gets each other off.

Until and only when I, the bottom, place trust in the top . . . the bottom always rules. A top will ask what me what I've done, what I want to do, and what my "threshold at present" is. A "threshold" can mean such fun objectives like extending the length of time that I suffer or endure an edging; my nipples worked over; my genitals electroshocked; or my pecs flogged. As you see, it is my ability to tolerate pain that is paramount. Guaranteed that my getting a little stoned, having my nipples worked over, and my pecs flogged will send me into the stratosphere of an endorphin rush. Just imagining such a scene will stiffen my resolve, leaving me spent. The top, now having his innate erotic need to dominate a twisted muscle stud bottom fully satisfied, also achieves orgasm. Hearing a top say to me at the conclusion of our scene, "You've given everything that I've asked for," leaves me with a warm feeling for the guy.

ROBERT: For me to go to a dungeon, it would have to be somebody that I knew pretty well over an extended period of time for me to develop the level of trust. I have a fear factor of being tied up or somehow restrained in a way that I can't get out and not knowing what that person is going to do to me.

JESSAY: Being in a dungeon doesn't mean that you're gonna always be tied up. There's this notion that it's about fear and losing control, but it's actually not like that. There's a lot of trust involved and a lot of protocols for protection, which can make it all very tender.

MICK: Exactly, that's why you discuss all prior to what's going to happen. You know, a little grass helps, a little red wine, a little smooth talking. There can be an element of romance that I find very scintillating. Usually, these are very interesting guys.

BILL: I have never experimented in that particular world. I'm very vanilla. Passionate vanilla.

MICK: The only time when I felt out of control was in an isolation chamber. Freestanding and built like a bank vault, though it was padded. In soft black leather! Which is good because when the door was shut the chamber went pitch-black. I could not see a hand in front of my face. Unless a two-way speaker was activated, no one could hear me. In less than a minute, I'd thrown my body against all four sides. There were little holes and vents where inhalants and clouds could be pumped in. The host was savage. He just waited. At last the little slit in the door opened. Calmly, he asked, "How you doing, Mick?" In a low and I admit desperate voice I replied, "Sir, please let me out!" He was cruel. Still, I was in the grasp of a hot dom top daddy!

JESSAY: That's why we're all not the same. I try not to judge you.

MICK: When you say that you can't handle being blindfolded, that means you are unwilling to give up the control. You have to know how far you want to go with somebody. What is the extent of and how strong is your mutual trust? Because pain and its high are temporary. Hey, I'm a freak . . . a pain pig. Yes, I experience discomfort and hurt. That's part of the training. But no injury for me. That's my rule. By the way, if you're wrapped up in plastic, that kind of confinement is torture.

IS THERE ANYTHING YOU WON'T DO?

MICK: I won't do scat. I won't do blood. I won't do piss . . . but anything else goes.

JESSAY: Water sports are degrading to me. But I look at everything through a racial lens, which nobody here would understand. It's just demeaning to me.

ROBERT: I had a couple of encounters with a guy who was into water sports. He wanted me to piss on him and piss up at his ass and all kinds of things. And I did it. But only as a top.

JESSAY: Bill is shook. He can't speak.

BILL: I'm pretty clean.

WHAT'S YOUR BIGGEST TURN-ON?

BILL: I have two things that will basically prove my last point: one, if they're attractive to me—which is pretty loosely defined since attractiveness can take many guises; and secondly, if they're nice. Kindness is sexy. Those two things absolutely make me melt.

ROBERT: The very first thing that I react to when I see someone is whether or not they have a cute ass. I like a sculpted, muscular bubble butt.

MICK: Super-heavyweight-class bodybuilders, like a Mr. Olympia. That's my fetish.

JESSAY: Kissing. It starts the whole thing for me. If somebody doesn't kiss, I ain't gonna be with you. Bad breath is the worst. And when they come in at you with just tight lips—uh-uh, nothing happening there.

WHAT MORE CAN YOU SAY ABOUT KISSING?

JESSAY: You need to know how to do it. You need to practice in a mirror like I did when I was young. I practiced with Vaseline and made lip marks on the mirror to make sure that they were formed right.

BILL: To me, you know, sex, when it happens, it's a minute and that's it. But kissing and cuddling to me are the most important part of sex. But I agree with Jessay, when they come at you with just tight lips, I mean, that's the worst.

ROBERT: I have found myself in situations where a guy that I was playing with would want to do a lot of intense kissing, and I wasn't really into him that much. You go along with the program but try to end it as soon as possible.

MICK: I like a good, wet French kiss. Or when the guy smokes from a bong and takes in a big, big toke. He embraces me. Then I open my mouth, close my eyes, and WHAM! There is this incredible breath exchange. We both look at each other and exclaim, "Medicated!"

BILL: Shotgunning is the most wonderful feeling in the world. I love kissing.

ROBERT: To me, kissing is an indication of a stronger kind of relationship with a person. It's very intimate. I've realized in my self-analysis that because my last lover/relationship was such an awful breakup, that it has literally affected the way I relate to people ever since. And if I find that there's someone who is really interested in me, I have a self-defense mechanism in which I pull away from that person and don't want to kiss them—which feels too vulnerable. I won't get together with them again, because I don't want to lead them into a place I'm not willing to go.

BILL: I get it. I echo everything Bob just said. My last relationship, fifteen of sixteen years were good. But then the last year was so bad that I built up a self-defense mechanism. I don't let people get close to me—and that means not letting someone kiss me. And it's not something I try to do. It's something that's ingrained in me now.

MICK: If you want a real tell-all, when I know that a guy is interested in me, it's when he rims me really good. Rimming is the penultimate experience. There's a difference between a guy who has a fetish for rimming and when the guy is, like, really interested in you. That's when he wants to drive you crazy.

JESSAY: I never make a first move. It's a fear of rejection. So everybody comes to me, and I'll reject them. I don't like it, but I still will talk to people I meet. I'm really about getting to know the person. Not all the time. 'Cause sometimes you just need to get it now. It's different with each person. But I have become freer because of listening to their stories. Never say never. That's what I've learned. I try to be open.

HAS BEING IN THE OLD GAYS MADE YOU THINK ABOUT DOING THINGS YOU NEVER WOULD HAVE DONE BEFORE?

BILL: No, Mick's stories reinforce my vanilla-ness. In the heat of passion, things have happened. I mean, I'm so hot for this guy that I would just do anything for him. Those situations pop up.

MICK: It's okay to make a fool of yourself. It's okay to be vulnerable. I guess maybe that's because of my training as an actor. You have to stay vulnerable here, inside. And still develop a thick skin to handle the criticism. Just like every human being has or will. I've been hurt many times, too. That's part of the game. In the great scheme of things, very few people have a better-than-average win-loss record. Most of us have a losing record. You have to forgive yourself. For foolishness. For having made the wrong choice. Otherwise, you dry up.

WHAT'S YOUR BODY COUNT?

MICK: I don't know how many notches.

JESSAY: I've never even thought about it.

BILL: That's a very straight thing, I think.

ROBERT: I have sat down and thought about how many men I have come in contact with, particularly since I moved to the desert. In my first twenty years here, I was very active. Based on the rate I had, I estimate that I played around with something on the order of five thousand different men.

BILL: Those are Wilt Chamberlain numbers.

MICK: I wager most people alive . . . do not know who Wilt Chamberlain was.

JESSAY: My heart gets too involved, so my numbers are low.

MICK: I was partnered for twenty-five years of my life. I didn't have a lot of contact with the outside. After we'd separated and then divorced, let's just say I made up for lost time. I think that's how we described back it in the 1970s. I didn't care who. I didn't remember who. I just gorged myself at the continuous bacchanal.

ROBERT: When I broke up with my first partner, all of a sudden it was 1980, and I was in San Francisco. I was wild. That could be a book in and of itself.

BILL: When you throw in the bathhouses . . .

Bill at three months old with
his parents in Westwood,
California, in 1944

Bill posing for his partner's
oil portrait in Laguna Beach,
California, in 1965

Bill

Bill atop Haleakalā Crater in Maui, Hawaii, in 1983

Jessay at two years old with his sister after church in Greeneville, Tennessee, in 1955

Jessay's high school senior yearbook photo, 1971

Jessay

Jessay going out on the town in drag to see Sheryl Lee Ralph in Los Feliz, California, in 1997

Mick with his grandmother at Lake Vermilion in Minnesota in 1959

Mick at thirty-eight years old at a professional photo shoot in Los Angeles, California, in 1994

Mick's high school senior yearbook photo, 1974

Robert

Robert at five years old, cutting his birthday cake in Jonesboro, Arkansas, in 1948

Robert's high school senior yearbook photo, 1961

Robert on a Sunday afternoon at a lake in Golden Gate Park in 1983

Bill at one of Robert's debaucherous infamous dinner parties

Robert and Bill beaming from ear to ear at the 2021 amfAR Gala in Los Angeles, California, mostly because they're in the same room as Madonna

Backstage with Drew Barrymore after a taping of her show in September 2021

Filming a brand partnership video for Savage X Fenty
in February 2022

Our first trip to the Hollywood sign as
a group, in March 2022

Filming a brand partnership
video for Walgreens at the house
in May 2022

On set with Jennifer Hudson at a taping of her show in January 2023

Taking time to enjoy the California lifestyle

Robert does some woodworking at sunset

Jessay and Mick, always laughing it up

JESSAY: Those don't count. I went to a bathhouse exactly one time. I had a headache, and I thought my friends gave me aspirin, but it was speed. I remember absolutely nothing. When I came out of it, I said, "You're not friends." I was so excited about going and so nervous. I said, "What did I do?" They said I just sat there and ran my mouth.

IS THERE SUCH A THING AS TOO MUCH MASTURBATION?

MICK: Absolutely not.

BILL: What it does is, it takes all the angst away and all of a sudden everything is nice again. That's the way I describe it. It takes the angst away from you.

JESSAY: It helps me to fall asleep.

ROBERT: I have a belief that masturbation on a regular basis is a very important thing to maintain the health of your body.

MICK: I beat off every day, every moment, every stroke. I have a complete ritual. I get stoned. I have a football game on mute. My computer plays multiple slideshows of bodybuilders. I play some really wild, deep techno music. It takes about an hour. I have multiple orgasms. Then I tell the guys about my latest ejaculation. Down to the smallest detail.

ROBERT: He makes the most incredible noises—a cross between intense pleasure and pain. And sometimes I'm not sure if I need to go in and pick him up off the floor.

WHAT'S YOUR FAVORITE PORN GENRE?

MICK: There's a label I really like called Centurion. Muscle guys up in San Francisco. Nice bodies, really heavy action.

BILL: Bob turned me onto Chaturbate. You open up the screen and there are forty different thumbnails of guys doing stuff in one big room. You pick your favorite and it links to his camera and you see what he's doing. Then you can go back and go to another person.

ROBERT: It's live-action. A lot of them are by themselves and it's just a jerk-off or an ass.

MICK: There are a lot of straight guys who do crossover, gay for pay.

JESSAY: Do you like a little story in your porn?

BILL: The acting is so bad. I just want to get into it. It's like, shut up.

MICK: I do screen a lot of porn. That's where you get the best ideas. Also, you pick up tips and follow good techniques.

WHAT'S YOUR SIGNATURE MOVE?

MICK: They always ask me to flex my biceps, pecs, and back. I have a routine that I constantly work on so I can improve each time. It helps to set the mood.

JESSAY: I don't have one.

MICK: I love dirty talk.

BILL: I like it to a point. I mean, and a lot of guys have said, "Oh, can you be my daddy?" No, I don't want to talk about being your daddy.

MICK: When the hot young studs ask me to be their daddy, I love that. What sends me up high is, I meet up with a mutant-sized muscled dom in a cruisy leather bar. He is in uniform or leather. You know, with a cap and a handlebar mustache. He walks up to me. It's, like, really dark. In a low almost whisper, he starts talking dirty and trash. He works me into one of the bar's dark corners, pushing me to the wall. That's where the two of us start . . .

ROBERT: Dirty talk is a little difficult for me for some reason. But I do express sounds of joy.

JESSAY: I like it if it's serious. If it's made-up, no. If it's forced, no.

BILL: I just find it to be corny and silly.

ROBERT: It's not something I do naturally.

DO YOU LIKE COSTUMES OR ROLE-PLAYING?

BILL: Underwear shows.

JESSAY: I will say leather; even putting it on makes my voice go down low. It's the smell of leather. I do give up the sissy and become a little more butch. But, see, I get embarrassed. But I can't turn red like y'all.

MICK: I like rubber. Especially when in Europe, in England, going to bars and seeing guys who dress in rubber. I don't really pull it off. But it's really hot to me. Of course, I like leather, and superhero costumes.

JESSAY: It's a joke to me to see furries, with the animal costume wagging his tail.

MICK: Puppy play? The way it's done, it can be hot. It's a jock thing, too. You put on a dog mask made of soft leather. They stick a plug in your butt and you're tied up in a harness. Black leather mitts are tied on your hands. You walk on all fours. You follow commands. The best puppy play that I've seen was in Berlin. Berlin is pure theater.

HAVE YOU EVER TRIED TANTRIC SEX?

MICK: Yeah. Every time I've begun what I was led to believe was a tantric scene. It turns out to be a scene with somebody who really wants to blow clouds with you.

ROBERT: People who smoke meth can go for a really long time. I'm too impatient for that.

HICKEYS—YEA OR NAY?

ROBERT: Early in my sexual life, I would get hickeys on my neck all the time.

JESSAY: I've done it. Not purposefully. I'm just getting that this is my spot to go into and I just will stay there on somebody. But then I'll realize what's happening. Have you ever gone to work with one?

BILL, MICK, ROBERT: Yes.

JESSAY: I went around church college, mind you, with this, but dark skin helps.

BILL: I just wore high collars.

ROBERT: That's when you become a cowboy.

MICK: I don't like it when that happens, and I know when somebody has done it. To me that's really forward.

BILL: To me, it's not sensual. Somebody's just trying to put their mark on you. I don't like that.

JESSAY: Sometimes I just am so into somebody, it just happens.

MICK: Then you're running around for the next day, frantically taking a cold spoon to your neck.

BILL: To me it's too much like high school, where kids used to do it just for the attention.

DOES SIZE MATTER?

ALL: Yes!

ARE YOU A TOP, BOTTOM, VERSE, ALL OF THE ABOVE, SOME OF THE ABOVE, OR OTHER?

BILL: I'm versatile.

ROBERT: I am primarily top but versatile.

JESSAY: I am a bottom right now because I had prostate cancer and the treatment is temporarily affecting my performance. That's the only reason, because I like being versatile.

MICK: Mostly bottom. And size matters. That's the beauty of dating apps like Scruff or Grindr, you know right off. Guys like to send me pics and video of them having fun.

DO YOU LIKE SENDING OR RECEIVING DICK PICS?

JESSAY: I have no problem receiving, but I don't share. It takes a lot for me to share. I tell guys, one time you say hi to me without any kind of picture, I say, "Face pic." If it's not the next time, I block you.

BILL: The dick pics I have don't have my face in them.

MICK: In the early '90s, I did a photo shoot with a graphic artist who shot black-and-white nudes. You know, physiques. There was full frontal nudity. I had already given up acting as a career, so I didn't care. My partner expressed no opposition. We were invited to the opening at a very swank La Brea Avenue gallery. The funny part was when acquaintances and friends, people who knew me only within the context of our relationship, found out I was one of the models, they looked and talked to me in an altogether different way. I had to ask them to put their tongues back in their mouths. At least for the remainder of the event.

ROBERT: Jeff Stryker, the famous porn actor, is the one who made a famous dildo fashioned out of his own penis and balls.

MICK: You know Circus of Books on Santa Monica Boulevard in West Hollywood? My partner was in the store, and he was making a purchase. Also standing in line was Jeff Stryker. He was carrying three of the Jeff Stryker–brand dildos. After Jeff had placed the three items on the counter and the cashier had rung up the total, the cashier said, "That'll be $200." Jeff Stryker takes out this big ledger and writes out a business-sized check for the dildos. From the ledger Jeff tears the draft out. He hands the check over to the cashier, who examines the check and its signature. In a loud voice the cashier says to Jeff Stryker, "Hmmm. I'll need identification, please." The entire store broke out laughing.

BILL: That's funny because in our design showroom, we had one salesman who was really flamboyant. He brought a client down, sat at the desk, and the client gave him a check. And it was from Jeff Stryker's mom. He looked at the check and saw Stryker and realized who she was. They looked at each other and immediately started laughing.

ROBERT: The guy got around.

JESSAY: He did a film at my friend's place in San Francisco. I didn't have an interaction.

MICK: I met him once at a party. Actually, he's a very sweet man. And it is *that big.*

WHAT'S YOUR FAVORITE SEX TOY?

JESSAY: My sling.

MICK: I have a hood. I have a mask. I have a Mongolian ball gag. I have crops. I have many different kinds of anal toys, in many different shapes and colors and weights.

ROBERT: Some of them are electronic.

BILL: They have new ones now where, like, if you're going on Chaturbate, the guy has a thing up his butt and you can activate it online by signal.

ROBERT: The viewer can control how intense or gradual the vibration of the butt plug will be.

MICK: Here's a question: How many people in this room have lost a vibrator stuck up their ass?

JESSAY: Next question!

WHAT'S YOUR MOST EMBARRASSING SEX STORY?

ROBERT: In college at Washington University, one time, probably about my third or fourth year, I had an eye infection. It was swollen and itching. I didn't know what it was. So I went to the health center and they looked and they said, "You need to go to an eye doctor at the medical center." I remember I was in this totally dark room sitting in the middle of the room. The eye doctor with the magnifying equipment was looking to try to see the problem. And after a moment, he said, "Oh my God. Oh my God. Do you mind if I have someone else look at this?" I said of course because it was a research hospital. There must have been twenty interns and doctors who, one after another, came in and looked at my eye. They all reacted in the same fashion, total shock. Finally, they told me I had crab eggs in my eye. I was embarrassed as hell.

JESSAY: I did have something happen. It wasn't embarrassing. It was scary. My partner and I had gone to beautiful San Francisco and we got a room in this nice hotel, had a great time. And then he goes back home, because at the time he was married. He calls me up and says, "Are you itching?" And I go, "Itching?" He goes, "Yeah, in your pubic hair." I was. We had lice. I felt like the nastiest person.

BILL: In San Francisco they had little buttons that said "Check 44" because 44 Hunt Street was the public health department where everyone went when they got gonorrhea. And I was there many times. I've also had crabs many times.

WHAT'S YOUR FAVORITE POSITION?

BILL, MICK, ROBERT: Doggy style!

JESSAY: I love to make out when I'm having sex.

MICK: Because of my neuropathy I'm limited with the type of positions. It really does impact, you know, because I like it very athletic.

ROBERT: I like to play around with different positions, but doggy style is my favorite. And I also really like outdoor settings. There's something very sensual about it.

WHERE'S THE WILDEST PLACE YOU'VE HAD SEX? AND WHERE'S THE DREAM SPOT?

ROBERT: I have two places. One of which was on top of the cyclotron at Washington University. I was working for PhD candidate researchers, so I had a key to get into the cyclotron room whenever I wanted. It's a big circular machine, and it shoots particles. I'd brought a guy I'd picked up cruising in the park. We went down to the room housing the machine, climbed up on top of it, and did the dirty. Fortunately, it was idle at the time. I've also had a few casual encounters with guys at night on the roof of the house where I lived, and we'd play up there. It was like being onstage—you could see the traffic and people below, but they couldn't see you.

MICK: The most unusual place that I've had sex was at the Gare d'Austerlitz, the train station in Paris. My ideal place would be Batman's lair. Oh, I'm hot to play Batman . . .

BILL: What about Robin?

MICK: I'm not a Robin fan, but I suppose I could play Batman or Robin. It would be fun, and when it's over Alfred brings you drinks.

BILL: Sex on the beach is wonderful, so on a beach in the South Pacific would be my ideal. I'd rather see a guy in a Speedo than naked.

JESSAY: I know where I would like to have sex: on the front deck of a large cruise ship. I'd want to be outside and feel the air going around me on the ship. I haven't had sex in an unusual or weird place. Basically, I'm a vanilla in bed person. I really am. Because I like my comfort.

ROBERT: I'd love to have sex on the Eiffel Tower.

WHO IS YOUR DREAM LOVER?

ROBERT: Shawn Mendes. He's got a great lean body. And a full head of hair. Being bald, I find myself really being drawn to people who have thick heads of hair. Another guy that I wouldn't mind getting it on with that we met fairly recently is Colton Underwood from *The Bachelor*. He is a very nice-looking guy. And friendly. We were even trying to do a collab with him.

MICK: Austin Wolf, the porn star.

BILL: Ricky Martin because I have a soft spot in my heart for Latino men.

JESSAY: Marvin Gaye. He exuded sensuality. He looked like someone who would actually give you love and not just want it. He exuded love. I want it just like that. Gentle. I'm such a romantic.

9

THE AIDS CRISIS

"My Circle Is Gone."

We had the time of our lives during the sexual revolution and gay liberation era of the '60s and '70s. We'd lived through so much rejection, repression, and discrimination in our early lives. Finally we were free to express ourselves, to live openly, to feel safe(r), and to connect with people without fear of persecution. We'd found support, love, friendship, and community. By the 1980s this newly won opportunity for a free and open life came crashing down around us. The public health crisis began with an article in the *New York Times* that described a rare skin cancer found in multiple cases involving homosexual men and centering in New York City. Like a California wildfire, the cancer—Kaposi sarcoma—spread fast. Soon gay men in all the major cities were being hospitalized for a variety of "opportunistic diseases" not seen in otherwise healthy patients. The epidemic was spreading throughout the country.

Until HIV (Human Immunodeficiency Virus) was discovered, and the life-threatening ailments we came to know of today as AIDS (Acquired Immunodeficiency Syndrome) were identified, the climate was uncertain, the public was in a full panic, and in our leaders, fear had replaced courage. Sound familiar? Look at the above words "human" and "virus," which in large part describe the pandemic. There are not the words "gay" and "plague." HIV is a retrovirus, meaning it cannot live outside the human body. When exposed to the air it lasts about ninety seconds. Bleach obliterates it.

Thankfully, medicine has created effective treatments that prevent HIV from spreading in the body. Pharmaceuticals are so successful that the amount of HIV in the blood is undetectable, meaning HIV cannot then be transmitted from one human host to the next. HIV is transmissible only from blood to blood, or body fluid to fluid. This is important because before HIV was even identified, public health officials had closed the bathhouses in New York City and San Francisco.

In retrospect this was a colossal mistake. History tells us that the bathhouses were a critical gateway into the gay community. A place to educate sexually active gay men to get regularly tested for HIV and to practice safe sex. Meaning to refrain from anal sex or wear a condom. And for that matter, not to share needles.

Instead, within this climate of fear and ignorance the bathhouses had become an easy target, symbolic of what a still homophobic society had come to think as public debauchery. To the San Francisco gay community, having sex was freedom of expression. The shuttering of the bathhouses was a retreat from freedom. At city hall, we protested outside then-mayor Dianne Feinstein's office clad only in our towels, shouting, "Out of the tubs and into the streets!"

People living with HIV and those who have died from AIDS have come from all of humanity's diversity. We are your children, brothers and sisters, parents, friends, lovers, and companions, and we have suffered. "Before AIDS, everybody had this naive optimism that we were going to waltz into equality," Mick says. "Like this wasn't going to be a struggle. Like this wasn't going to be, you know, as dark as it really turned out to be, and for a long time." It's not that we didn't struggle prior to our liberation. But liberation, like all social progress, is precarious. We should never take our freedoms for granted.

In the gay community, this was about to be tested in fatal ways. The AIDS epidemic decimated our community and had a lasting impact on gay men everywhere. It changed our lives irrevocably, especially Robert's and Mick's. The two are very open about the fact that they are HIV+ and have lived to tell the tale. All the Old Gays hope their openness can help to destigmatize living with HIV, and inspire anyone else who has it, or any other incurable disease, to make the life-affirming choices absolutely necessary for survival and, thus, to thrive.

BILL: "I LOST 80 PERCENT OF MY FRIENDS."

At the end of 1979, one day after work I decided to stop by the Castro and have a drink. It was on that day that I met my partner of the next sixteen years. Love sometimes happens when you're least expecting it. I was just out having a good time, and boom, it hit me. My new boyfriend lived on a houseboat in Sausalito, and after eight months of dating, he asked me to move in, effectively removing me from the gay scene in the city. We had a monogamous relationship. He's the reason I'm alive. I wouldn't be here if I hadn't met him.

In the early '80s, I worked in Showplace Square, which was the design center in San Francisco. The first time I heard anything about a scary new disease was in March 1980. I found out that a salesperson in another showroom across the street had died of "gay cancer." It wasn't called AIDS yet. I didn't know what to say. It was the first time I'd ever heard the phrase.

Shortly after that, Randy Shilts started writing a daily article in the *San Francisco Chronicle* following a Muni worker who lived in Twin Peaks. His neighbors saw him falling and started helping him walk down the street to work. Randy was quite controversial later on, during the plague, because he wanted to close the bathhouses. Guys who were used to freewheeling sex in San Francisco took a big offense to it. But the truth of the matter was, a lot of unsafe sex was happening in the bathhouses.

In the beginning everyone was confused. We read Randy's and Herb Caen's columns and Armistead Maupin's serialized "Tales of the City" in the *Chronicle* every single day for any crumb of information.

It all just snowballed. I lost 80 percent of my friends. That figure might seem high, but I was working in the design district, where almost everyone was gay. So it really hit us hard there. One of the saddest deaths I can remember was an employee we had named Jim. He was twenty-one, tall and good-looking. He had a dancer's body, and he entertained everyone, goofing around, pulling fabrics around him like they were dresses, that kind of thing. Everybody loved Jim. And then he got it. One night, a group of us decided to visit him in the hospital. The only way that I could interact with Jim was to hold his hand and ask him a question. If the answer was yes, he'd press against my hand once. If the answer was no, he'd press it twice. To see this handsome guy who was now emaciated and couldn't even talk, that's what killed me. He was talented. He had his whole life in front of him. To die that young?

The hardest part of it for me was when my friends were afraid to tell me they had AIDS because of the stigma. One time I saw an ex-boyfriend at Macy's buying pajamas. I immediately thought, *Oh my God, he's come down with it, and he'll be bedridden, so he's buying pajamas.* Sure enough, I heard not long after through friends he'd died of AIDS.

It seemed that I was going to memorial services month after month. Going to memorial services was just something that you did. I can't tell you how many times I heard "Candle in the Wind," the

Elton John song. Literally every funeral played it. Every time I heard it, tears would fall down my face. By the time I'd been to dozens of funerals, the song actually made me cry tears of laughter, in a dark humor kind of way.

The conversations I had with my friends who were still alive were all about recounting who had just died. We talked about it matter-of-factly. We also talked about being terrified to hook up. Some of us were being very careful about who we dated and to not automatically end up having sex. Kissing was even out because the transmission of saliva was one of the simplest ways to get it. If you were a bottom and your partner enjoyed oral sex, there was a big commotion about, "Hey, can you get AIDS by having oral sex with someone or does it happen in another way?" The bottom line was that the quickest way was to have intercourse with someone.

Despite the fear of impending doom and growing knowledge about the disease, a lot of my friends were still running around. Sex to them was more important than anything else, and they were in denial. In the beginning, when you found out someone died, it was very sad. But as the disease progressed into the '90s, instead of feeling sorry for people, you kind of wondered why they didn't have better sense to protect themselves and others. There was a lot of passing judgment.

Another common thing that happened was that once someone had contracted AIDS, and they resigned to the fact that they were going to die, they ran up their credit cards. They wanted to enjoy the last part of their lives. Once you got that diagnosis, it was a death sentence, and you didn't know how much time you had. It could be a month; it could be a year.

During that time, I went to Kauai and ran into an old friend on the beach. I asked him how he was doing and he said sadly, "Not too well. I found out I have AIDS." As soon as he did, he moved to Hawaii because that's where he wanted to die. A lot of people sold all their stuff and minimized their lives to prepare for death. I lived in Guerneville, above San Francisco, for a year, and there were a lot of HIV+ people who rented a cabin there up in the mountains and passed away there. They just didn't want to be around anybody. No one was seeing a way out.

Being in a monogamous relationship, I felt fortunate and safe but I wanted to help in some way. So I took an intensive course to become a certified massage therapist at a school in Oakland called Body Electric, an organization at the forefront of the AIDS epidemic. Body Electric volunteers gave free massages to AIDS patients. We learned how to maneuver around a hospital bed, avoid lesions, and make the person feel most comfortable. To many, they were considered pariahs, so to give them caring human touch gave me good peace of mind. I really enjoyed giving massages.

In 2003, toward the end of the height of the AIDS crisis, I moved down to Palm Springs after my partner and I broke up. A lot of guys were trying to hook up with me, but there was an unspoken rule that HIV+ people don't try to pick up negative people. There were still people getting AIDS. I admit I wasn't really an angel during this time, and I learned a big lesson the hard way.

I went on a telephone line called Confidential Connection, where you dialed a number and you'd hear the voices of all these guys describing themselves. If you wanted to talk to one, you'd leave a message and then you could talk further and exchange numbers. I met a very nice man, and he told me he was negative, so we had unsafe sex, which I did not do that often, but it did happen every once in a while. He also told me he had been in prison, where he got the nickname "Freedom" because he was so nice, everyone knew he was going to get out early.

We went together for about twelve months, and at some point during that time, I found out his previous lover had died of AIDS. Meanwhile, a friend of mine was a nurse, and she had treated my boyfriend. She would always say to me, "Bill, are you being careful? You really should be careful." But she couldn't say anything detailed because of patient confidentiality.

One afternoon, my new lover and I went to a company picnic together, and he went home because he wasn't feeling well. I thought he had the flu. I called the nurse friend and asked what I should give him.

"Bill, ask him if he has AIDS," she begged me.

I asked him if he was HIV+. He said yes. Turned out he had full-blown AIDS.

"Why didn't you just shoot me?" I cried. "How could you do this to me?"

"I didn't think we were going to be a big deal," he replied. "Then I really fell for you and I really didn't want to say it because I liked you so much and didn't want to lose you."

I went to an urgent care and got tested. I waited two weeks.

It was the longest two weeks of my life.

I finally got my letter. I opened it up . . . I was still negative. I could have done backflips because I had already started to think what my life was going to be living with AIDS. That relationship ended, and in my self-admonishment for putting myself at risk, I was forced to consider my earlier judgments of others. I thought to myself, *How could I have been so stupid?* And then I thought, *I'm no different from anyone else.* I was ashamed of myself for doing it, but it made me understand everyone else's dilemma very clearly.

ROBERT: "THE ONLY EQUIVALENCY I CAN THINK OF IS WARTIME, WHERE A SOLDIER MIGHT LOSE THEIR ENTIRE TROOP."

We were living in San Francisco when it hit; we were at ground zero. At the very beginning, on a daily basis, I would go down to the Castro and have breakfast at one of the restaurants there, either with my roommates or with a friend, and we'd chitchat. There was a gay newspaper in the city called *BAR*, the *Bay Area Reporter*, which came out weekly. It was a pretty good newspaper because it would report on stuff happening in the gay community. We started seeing little articles about an unexplained illness that was cropping up in San Francisco and New York. "Have you heard about this gay cancer?" someone asked me. "It's only affecting gay men." That was my first inkling that something was happening.

San Francisco became one of the epicenters. In the early '80s, I was working as a city planner, specifically directing a study to determine whether or not it was feasible to build a new stadium near downtown for the San Francisco Giants, which resulted in the ballpark we see today. I was in Mayor Dianne Feinstein's office a lot. Dianne had a liaison to the gay community, a guy by the name of Chuck Forrester, who I had known casually and got to know better. We'd talk a lot about HIV from the perspective of the responsibilities that fell to the mayor's office. The bathhouses were controversial. When the mayor's office closed them down, half of the gay community was furious and the other half applauded her. I frequented the bathhouses a lot, and like a lot of gay guys in the beginning, I was not happy that the powers that be wanted to close them down. Before you knew it, they were gone.

There wasn't a lot of information about AIDS at first. You'd go out to the bars, and they would be as crowded as ever. People were still picking up tricks and taking them home. I mean, it wasn't something that any of us could have imagined, so it was hard to react to what was a real and yet still abstract threat. We still weren't entirely clear on how it spread.

We'd keep talking about it because it was afflicting more and more people. Then by 1982, *BAR* started publishing who'd died the previous week. It started out being a short list, then it grew and kept growing until it was a column. Every week you'd go down the names and you would see more and more people you knew.

It hit me hard at a very personal level. When I first moved to San Francisco, I moved in with two guys who helped me with a renovation.

They both died. I dated a guy named Phillip. He died. I dated a guy named John. He died. I ran around with a group of friends. I would say there were a dozen of us who would get together every few weeks and we'd party at somebody's house. And every single male in that group died except for me and one other guy, named Lloyd, who was a nurse. He's still alive and living in Florida.

Paralyzing fear gripped me as I witnessed my entire circle of friends dying around me, one after the other. It took me until 1987 to work up enough nerve to get the test. I could have been infected in the early '80s, for all I knew. But I was scared to test, and I finally just got to the point where I said, *I really have to know.* Lloyd helped me out. He acted as an intermediary between my doctor and me. I had my blood taken, and it took about a week to get the results. Frankly, I didn't expect it to be positive because I had no signs or anything. And then Lloyd came by the house one day and he said, "Well, I've got your results . . . and they're positive." He said it very matter-of-fact. I was immediately frozen.

I'll never forget the day I was diagnosed, almost seven years to the day after I first heard of AIDS. When I moved to San Francisco, I had an image of what I wanted. I wanted to live in this beautiful city and renovate a house on top of a hill that had a hot tub in the living room, where I could sit and look out over the city while drinking wine and smoking a joint. Those were heady days. I was chumming around with the mayor and the heads of the utilities and banks, going to the yacht club for dinner, and going to Giants baseball games using Robert Lurie's box. I had literally achieved everything I'd dreamed of, and it just got blown out of the water.

I was HIV+.

I was in a state of shock for four months. I was totally irrational, and panicky. Every little sore I'd get on my body led to a downward spiral. Unless you live through something like that, you really cannot comprehend what it's all about.

I finally snapped out of my catatonic state and started doing self-help-type programs. I took classes at San Francisco State University specifically for people who were HIV-infected. It was on meditation, relaxation therapy, and visualization therapy. It was a small class of maybe twelve to fifteen people, and we would meet for an hour every week.

The biggest thing I learned from that was the degree of control that the mind has over your physical body. That through visualization and concentration and focus, you can direct the energies within your body to deal with physical issues. Toward the end of the course, the instructor asked everyone to find something about your own body that you wanted to address. Don't tell anybody else, you're the only one to know. And we'd work on it over the next few sessions.

I had been dealing with plantar warts for several years prior, having them surgically removed with acid. I was trying everything, and they kept coming back. I thought, *Well, I'm going to focus on that.* He'd play the music and say, "Find your issue, then focus on it. Now try to relate it to something physical that you know and love and associate the two. So I associated my plantar wart with a flower. And I went through a process where over the next few sessions every time I looked at the bottom of my feet, instead of seeing the wart, I would see the bottom of my foot with a little flower. I would focus on that flower. It became a blooming flower with petals. Over time, it dried out, and the leaves withered and blew away. When they blew away, I no longer had a wart. They have not to this day returned.

I learned more than I realized at the time from that practice, and I think a lot of what I learned may have saved my life. Once I was able to function, I did an in-depth analysis of my life, what I wanted to do, where I wanted to be. I decided I did not want to die in San Francisco. AIDS was relentless throughout the '80s, and I had come to equate the city with death and suffering.

Having visited Palm Springs a few years before, I'd left with such good feelings about it that I immediately thought, *I'm going to move to the desert.* I decided I wanted to gear down my lifestyle. I was a city planner. I had my own consulting service, and I had good contacts. It was a good business, but I decided to put all of that aside and do something where I didn't have to account to anyone else what I was doing with my work time.

So, in early 1990, I moved to the Southern California desert. AIDS ultimately led to my life as an artist.

I came down to Palm Springs with the full expectation that I was going to be dead in a couple years. I was seeing my doctor monthly and getting a blood test. They monitored the viral load and my T-cell count, tests that became available in the late '80s. In 1989, my T-cell count had dropped below the average range, and my viral load was being measured in tens of thousands of particles. I knew from the data that I was on the pathway to death. Because back then, once your T cells dropped below two hundred, you were officially given an AIDS diagnosis. HIV status showed the presence of the virus but not necessarily the disease. AIDS was the expression that the virus was active.

I had a little bit of money at the time, a few hundred thousand dollars in the bank. And I spent rather recklessly. I would do a lot of eating out, barhopping, buying stuff. I had this thing for fancy little Italian sports cars. At one point I had three cars—a Chevrolet Blazer, a Lancia Zagato, and a silver Alfa Romeo Spider.

When I moved to the desert, I found a classic midcentury home in an area of Cathedral City called the Cove. I closed escrow on buying it the same day my San Francisco house closed escrow on its sale. I spent the next year and over $100,000 renovating it. The ceilings were popcorn, so I scraped all the ceilings. The floor was shag carpet. I pulled it up. I laid all the tile and did a lot of landscaping. That's the way I started blowing all my money.

When I first moved here and felt I was on a track toward death, I had a much more casual attitude about sex. It wasn't helping me. Then I really pulled back and made an assessment of my life. I asked myself seriously: *Okay, what do I need to do to make the best of whatever time I have left?*

I pulled back within myself. One of the pieces of advice that everyone with HIV/AIDS was told was to get the stress out of your life.

Part of my thought process was figuring out what the biggest stress was in my life. I concluded that it was dealing with other people. How could I avoid dealing with other people? The previous year spent renovating my house and making furniture for it had made me so happy. I loved working for myself, making and creating things from scratch.

I decided to put all my energy into being creative. I had a small back bedroom in my house, which I converted into a studio and started making small sculptural works. I started with a lamination technique using medium-density fiberboard material. One was a hand holding a tennis ball. Another became one of my most prized possessions, a self-portrait of sorts. I just looked at myself in the mirror and started creating a piece I called *Primal Scream*. It summed up how I felt inside, a physical manifestation of all the angst and frustration of living with an unpredictable, deadly disease.

After making art for a few months, I realized, *Hey, I can do this.* To this day I believe that channeling my energies into a positive experience was a very important element to my survival. When I did the meditation visualization workshops, I think a lot of those lessons became embedded in me. I removed myself from what I perceived to be a very negative, cloudy environment to the freedom of my life and the spiritually giving nature of the desert. It led to happiness. I believe I harnessed powers within me to a positive effect. And I believe those powers exist within every person, if they can only find a way to get to them, recognize, understand, and harness them.

I signed up with the Desert AIDS Project for regular monitoring of my health stats. I noticed that my T-cell count wasn't declining anymore, and my viral load was no longer increasing. A year and half after moving to Palm Springs, my T cells had climbed back above the lower end of the normal range, and my viral load was down into a barely detectable zone without having taken any kind of HIV medication. The desert had miraculously healed me.

I had a reckoning in 1991. My money was gone, and I thought, *Oh my God, I think I'm going to live, and I better do something about it.*

My best friend I had met in the desert, a guy named Larry Parks, introduced me to the owners of one of the gay resorts in Palm Springs who had bought another property they wanted to convert to a resort. They needed someone to landscape the grounds. I ended up working for them from 1992 to 1996. I was making art at a gay resort and meeting gay people. It also just happened to be in a hot spot for a lot of gay porn. So while I was working, the resort would be packed with gay porn stars. I'd observe all the filming going on and would offer my thought from time to time. They loved my artistic eye, and I became the go-to guy to landscape all the gay resorts' grounds in Palm Springs, including CCBC, the largest one in town, and the chain of four resorts owned by Rick Ford, creator of the legendary All Worlds Video.

For the next decade I was working in that environment, making pretty good money, and having fun. During that period of time—it was the mid–'90s—protease inhibitors came along. I was lucky enough to have access to them, and by around 2000, any thought of HIV was back of mind. I've been now undetectable for about eighteen years, with no viral load. I have high T-cell counts. HIV is the least of my problems. I am one of the few lucky ones—a real Cinderella story.

It took years to get to a place where sex seemed normal to me again. But this is the desert, a good place for sexual healing. I think that my health reversal has a lot to do with where I live. I think there are healing forces here that Native Americans have understood for generations.

Whenever I start thinking back on that harrowing time of my life, something triggers a memory of somebody and I'll think, *Why am I still alive?*

One permanent shift in my psyche, because I dealt with death so much, and I grieved so hard for so long, is to have become numb to people dying. At this point in my life, when I hear of someone who died, I just accept it without much feeling. Maybe that's denial, or maybe that's acceptance. I'm not sure. I feel much the same about my own mortality. When I try to process my own survival, I think logically and logistically, like, *Well, maybe I have a weaker strain of the virus.* That's one possibility. Another is more spiritual. I believe that what a person does in reaction to panic and fear can either drag them further down or, conversely, can help their immune system to fight.

Today, I'm very open about my HIV status. I don't consider it to be the mark of the devil or anything like that. Back in the '80s, during the turmoil, I had a very different perspective on it. I didn't want to be labeled as HIV+. In the end—and I can say this clearly because I was fortunate enough to survive—it was a blessing because it allowed for realizations I might not otherwise have had if I hadn't faced that kind of reality. Learning I was HIV+, and the changes I made as a result, was probably one of the best things to happen to me.

MICK: "I WAS IN THE WRONG PLACE, AT THE WRONG TIME, AND MADE A BAD CHOICE."

At first I was lucky. Other than having been infected with a strain of hepatitis B in early 1982, I dodged the bullet in several ways. In late 1979, I met Joel, who would become my partner for the next twenty-five years. When the tests first started coming out, I went to AIDS Project Los Angeles and had an anonymous test done and I came up negative. I needed to know because I was in a relationship. I guess I can credit my being with Joel all those years for keeping me negative for a long time.

At the height of the AIDS epidemic, I was going to a funeral once a month. The thing that I remember most about that time was going to the gym. One week you saw a person who looked pretty healthy, and then you never saw the guy again. I knew a lot of people who passed away. I stopped going to funerals because it was just too hard. If I started thinking about names, there would be many.

In 2001, I tested positive for HIV. Looking back, I was in the wrong place, at the wrong time, and made the wrong choice. From hard experience, I've learned that complete trust in a sexual partner is essential. Simply put, what I've learned is to forgive myself, and therefore I was able to forgive that individual. I mean, the first thing was to get better. The second thing was letting go of negative emotions. Being angry at yourself or at another person isn't going to help. You say, *This is what's happened,* and move on. Others may make their judgments. Not everyone has to know everything about you. Let them criticize what they *think* they know of you.

My first priority was staying healthy. By that time, a lot of medical advances had been made to treat and survive HIV. I mean, this was 2001, not 1991. And yet, my doctor at the time was very concerned. He'd prescribed AZT, and six months later I was very sick. That cut my hemoglobin by a quarter. I lost thirty pounds. I went from the high 190s to the low 160s. I thought, *Well, this isn't it.* My doctor had prescribed sulfonamides. It wasn't until later that I found out that I was allergic to sulfa. I had difficulty breathing and a painful rash. Thankfully, it was not serious enough to warrant a dreaded trip to the ER.

In January 2002 I attended an event sponsored by APLA (AIDS Project Los Angeles) with Gilead Sciences. The event promoted a new antiviral drug that had just been approved called Viread. After my doctors put me on that, my numbers dramatically improved. My viral load counts turned to undetectable. Unfortunately, rarely have my comprehensive T-cell counts reached above five hundred again. Somehow I've fended off but one serious disease (shingles), and for that I'm grateful.

Today, living with HIV for twenty-five years and single again for now sixteen years, I've had to rethink the concepts of hot sex, dating, and intimacy. It's a whole new world from what I experienced coming out in the 1970s. There's an oversized amount of misinformed and prejudicial judgment within our community. I've met a lot of guys, especially tops, who say to me: "Yeah, I only fuck negative men." I thought, *Okay, you plan on fucking men raw who tell you that they're negative and you think you're not at risk of being infected?*

To repeat: test. If your result is negative, or if you test positive and your viral load is undetectable, that means you are not at risk of transmitting HIV to another person.

If you're looking for unprotected sex? Have it with somebody who can prove they are undetectable because that is a guy you know is not going pass it on to you. But if you get into bed with somebody who has lied to you, or worse, doesn't know . . . that is a dangerous fantasy.

For safety, I assume that everybody *is* positive. From hard experience, I've learned that complete trust in a sexual partner is essential, but rarely does that happen. Boy, I wish we had dating apps twenty years ago. Now I can know of his HIV status, if he is taking PrEP or is undetectable. I've seen profiles where astute guys have posted their latest HIV test results and COVID-19 and monkeypox vaccinations. It's like any other interview. Ask questions and hope for an honest answer. It helps me decide if we are a potential match. Play will be safe or as close to it as possible.

Look, I don't want to be infected again. HIV mutates, and subsequent strains are more resistant to treatment. When the two of us agree to divulge our status, when we share the month and year of our last test, that's a green light.

What to Do If You're Scared of Getting AIDS

Thankfully, HIV is no longer a death sentence. Bob and Mick can attest to the effectiveness of their treatments, and they have survived for more than forty years and twenty years, respectively. Here is their best advice to staying healthy:

Know your status. Get tested to determine if you are HIV positive. You can do so in the privacy of your doctor's office, or at a site that tests anonymously. That means you are given a number or code and the result is matched to that number or code . . . not to any person by name. Go online or search on social media to find a doctor or testing sites near to you. Once you know your status, you can plan your life. And that's also the only way you're going to develop healthy relationships.

Seek treatment ASAP. If diagnosed with HIV/AIDS, go to a public health clinic or see your doctor. Do not dither—for your life and your family! However painful it might seem now, if you delay you will become sick. Remember that the objective of treatment is an HIV viral load count that is "undetectable."

Test. To keep your levels undetectable, you have to test.

Be careful dating. Know your partner's status. Find out as much as you can about your potential partner's sexual history before you roll around in the hay. Be strong in your convictions. Don't feel pressured to hook up with someone if you don't know their status. Here's a clue: honest people tend to stick around honest people, and liars hang out with liars.

Sign up for PrEP. That is "pre-exposure prophylaxis," a fancy term that means pills or shots that, when taken as prescribed by a doctor, have proven to be highly effective in preventing HIV.

Keep up on the latest treatments; they are always changing.

Take your meds as prescribed.

10
GAY MARRIAGE

I Do, But He Doesn't

The Old Gays have lots to say on the topic. Each of us have had different experiences and hold varied perspectives. One thing we have in common is that none of us ever believed in our lifetimes that marriage to another man would happen legally; it was inconceivable. We're happy to say that all of us have had passionate, loving long-term relationships. We've also been put through and survived the proverbial wringer of devastating breakups, divorce, and loss. As of this writing, each man's dating and social media profiles list them as "single," whatever that means. Thanks to ever-present Cupid and his arrow, that could change in a heartbeat! When it comes to matters of the crotch and heart, we never say never.

Here are our dramatic love stories. Read 'em and weep! Or at least say, "Aww."

MICK'S THE ONLY ONE
WHO MADE IT LEGAL

After moving to Laguna Beach, California, I had several of what we call "fuck buddies," punctuated by countless one-night stands. During the 1970s I had come to understand that if you saw a man for a month, in "gay years" that meant a year. Looking back, the six months John Tristram and I saw each other seemed like two years. Perhaps it was due to my being only twenty-three years old.

John was very good to me. Very good. He took me to my first gay pride parade, which happened to have been the first-ever pride parade held in West Hollywood. The festival was held on an asphalt parking lot behind the Pacific Design Center Blue Whale. Back then there were no red or green structures, no fountain, no public plaza, and no art gallery. At the festival, the faded, ripped, and torn blue jean–clad, bare-to-the-waist men were built, hot, and sexy. I mean, we are talking juiced, gym-built bodies. Arnold-sized pecs and tree-limbed thick and vascular biceps. The air was scented with man sweat, beer, and pot.

I was highly impressionable, open to the naughtiest of suggestion and most likely one of the youngest there. It wasn't that I'd been surrounded by dragons. Let's say this was a highly seasoned cohort of men. Gay men who dared to show up at a gay pride parade when many could have been evicted from their homes or fired from work. It was no small fact that at the other end of the asphalt parking stood the newly erected LA County Sheriff's Department West Hollywood station.

Although my tuition and fees at UC Irvine had been paid for over two years by scholarship, I had to get a job. By the second year of graduate school, I'd moved closer to campus, to an apartment in the back bay area of Newport Beach. My roommate was a young woman who thought it was a hoot that I was gay. That's because her first name was Gaye . . . Gaye Baldalf. She was wonderful.

I was hired at an upscale clothing store called JAM at nearby South Coast Plaza. One afternoon, a handsome man walked into the store. I sold him a belt, tie, and a pair of slacks, then he took me out for a fifteen-minute coffee break. It lasted forty-five minutes. His name was Joel Kimmel, and he introduced me to a new world.

Joel had been an actor. He'd played Linus in the first national tour of *You're A Good Man, Charlie Brown*, which took him from New York to Hollywood. A born comedian, Joel had teamed up with his co-star, Ann Gibbs, who'd played Lucy in *You're A Good Man, Charlie Brown*, performing stand-up comedy. Gibbs and Kimmel hit it big when one of their "on-spec" scripts, "A Girl Like Mary," was chosen for *The Mary Tyler Moore Show*.

By the time Joel took me out for coffee, Ann and he had already written scripts for such classic '70s TV shows as *The Jeffersons*, *Alice*, and *The Love Boat*. Thanks to Aaron Spelling's largesse, he'd just bought half of an exquisite 1920s Spanish two-story duplex adjacent to Fred Segal on Melrose Avenue. What really put me over the top was when Joel invited me to the annual Christmas party held by Norman Lear at the Beverly Hilton hotel. We'd only met the month earlier, in November. Gay years, remember? Now he was introducing me not only to Norman Lear but also to many people who would become constants in our twenty-five-year relationship.

Joel taught me so much. He taught me how to drive a manual transmission. He taught me basic Italian. Try as he did, he sought to instill in me comedic timing. How to tell a story and to make it pay off. One of Joel's most redeeming qualities was that he was extremely giving. His mother was blind, and when Joel was an actor in Hollywood, he used to volunteer as a reader at the Braille Institute. I think he still is very committed to volunteering, something I really didn't do.

We raised three golden retrievers, Roxy, Missy, and Ms. Hannah. And Rocky. Save for Roxy, who we'd raised from a puppy, Missy, Ms. Hannah, and Rocky were adopted. Rocky was a ninety-pound American foxhound Joel had introduced me to. Rocky belonged to a musician who had contracted AIDS. Joel volunteered to walk Rocky. He turned out to be my soulmate.

I believe that this was our greatest accomplishment—Roxy, Ms. Hannah, and Rocky lived well past fourteen years each. A lady lesbian friend of ours said, "When I come back, I want to be the pet animal of two gay men." Yes, they were our children.

People will tell you that Joel and I had fallen madly in love. I don't control what people say. Relationships are a day-to-day thing, I think. You have to work at it. Of my having lived for a quarter century in Hollywood? Well, there were distractions and relentless pressure.

Throughout lean years and very good years, we traveled together. Going to the theater on London's West End. Renting farmhouses in Tuscany, Umbria, and the Loire Valley. Hanging at a leather bar in Amsterdam or in Paris. Sunbathing and lunch in Cannes.

You want a celebrity story? In the 1980s, a fellow cast member of *You're A Good Man, Charlie Brown*, Jonathan Hadary, who'd played Schroeder, was in town and appearing in the LA production of *Torch Song Trilogy*. We met for a dinner along with other members of the cast. With them was Estelle Getty. Mrs. Getty had just won a Tony Award for her performance in the play. Over dinner she and Joel hit it off over their mutual love for the theater. Estelle looked to Joel for advice, he being a writer and executive story editor on numerous situation comedy television shows. In her autobiography, Estelle credits Joel for helping her prepare for the auditions and interviews that led to her being cast in the role of Sophia on *The Golden Girls*.

It has been said that *The Golden Girls*, Bea Arthur, Rue McClanahan, Betty White, and Estelle Getty, never went anywhere without a four-fag minimum. Well, that was so. Estelle had a devoted following. Good people with big hearts. It was a treat when Estelle, or "Ess-ie," invited us over for Sunday brunch. She'd make us matzo brei. The only dish she cooked.

Estelle and Rocky, our ninety-pound foxhound, hit it off, too. She'd come to the house, sit on the sofa. Rocky would walk right up to her, wagging his big tail. She'd say to all ninety pounds of him, "I dare you." He'd stretch out his neck, placing a big wet kiss on her mouth.

Only now do I see that Estelle and I share something. The applause and recognition that she and I both pursued did not come to us until our senior years. She was astute when it came to people, sizing everyone up as actors often do. And Estelle Getty did not suffer fools.

Now comes the hard part. I'm at a loss of pointing to one single crisis, event, or thought that precipitated Joel and me to break up. There are no protagonists in this part of our story. Only through couples therapy did I discover that a separation was needed. Instead, we agreed to split. Thank goodness that all of our doggy children had died.

It was not an amicable parting.

Before there was same-sex marriage in California, we had this experiment called "domestic partnerships." We applied, signing legal papers, and six weeks later a certificate arrived in the mail. Domestic partnerships were a way for us to further the commitment to our relationship. In that sense, I believe it worked because, after all, we'd been together for twenty-five years.

After a quarter of a century, I vacated the home that I shared with someone whom I still love. So many memories. Today it all seems like some dream. On my attorney's advice, I vacated our house taking only my clothing with me. To take other personal property out of the house could negate any claims I might have. After months of gut-wrenching accusations, argument, and nastiness we agreed to arbitration presided over by a retired family law judge. At that time domestic partnerships were under the jurisdiction of family court. To dissolve the partnership meant getting a divorce.

During arbitration I came to know the flaw within "domestic partnerships." California is a community property state. Yet there was little case law to justify my claim to "shared" property. That is why marriage equality is so important. It protects both parties and gives them equal standing in a court of law. Assets are divided 50/50. Had I possessed such standing, I believe our divorce would have been a clear and relatively easy negotiation.

A postscript

After our dissolution, I saw our couples therapist for a final session. I recall the therapist saying that in his experience it was rare for couples who had lasted so many years together to then end their relationship. If I were to do things differently, I would not have become so angry. Anger is hurt. Given the health crises that I've confronted these last years, I've had the support and time to own up to and work through my demons and shortcomings. And to see my strengths.

In hindsight I'm grateful that we made the domestic partnership, and I have no regrets. I wouldn't have done it any differently. I'm very proud that we were in the historic batch of the very first gay couples to have a legally binding "marriage" in the United States of America.

I truly believe the formality of the process promotes stability. When you must go through the legal system to dissolve the relationship, there's an emphasis on both of you to try as hard as you can to make it work. In my opinion, that's why same-sex marriage is so important for the LGBTQ+ community. It fosters healthier relationships and therefore healthier people. Bottom line is, I believe in the concept of marriage. Through marriage I think we treat each other a little better. I think there's a little more respect because of marriage.

Being a Doggy Daddy

I'm most grateful for having been a proud fur-baby father several times over. With Joel, we raised and rescued four special doggies. Our children whom we loved and shared together.

First, there was the brazen red-haired Roxy, who we raised from a puppy. We named her after the outrageous character Roxie Hart from the stage musical *Chicago*, and played by the equally fabulous redhead Gwen Verdon.

There was Ms. Hannah, whose great-grandparents were Liberty and Challenger, President Gerald R. and Betty Ford's golden retrievers. Ms. Hannah was a big girl, seventy-five pounds of red hair with beautiful golden accents. She was gorgeous, with the most fantastic feather-like tail. Ms. Hannah the banana was very "country club," with a very serious expression. She'd taken upon herself the duty to keep the three boys in her household—Joel, Rocky, and me—in line.

Between Roxy and Ms. Hannah, we'd adopted a platinum-colored, smaller-sized golden retriever named Missy. Sadly, we had Missy for only six months. She died from an aneurysm. That was very hard.

During that time, Joel had been elected to the board of PAWS (Pets Are Wonderful Support) Los Angeles. PAWS/LA is a wonderful support group for pet owners with HIV and other life-threatening illnesses. The nonprofit feeds, fosters, and pays for veterinary care of pet animals while their mommies and daddies are in the hospital or at home resting.

In our neighborhood in Hollywood we walked a ninety-pound American foxhound named Rocky. When it became clear that Rocky's owner was not going to survive, we signed an agreement with him promising to adopt his sweet boy. That's how Rocky came to live with us.

A volunteer at PAWS/LA himself, Rocky was the most magnetic and photogenic of dogs ever. He worked in volunteer orientation, and Rocky would greet them. Sitting and looking into each hooman's eyes, Rocky would put out a paw. He kept contact with that hooman and made sure that this new volunteer held on to his paw. For that moment, to Rocky, they were the most important person in the room. That is, until the next person came into the room and he left to go greet the new hooman.

For his efforts, Rocky was named a "volunteer of the year" by the city of West Hollywood in 1997. We took Rocky and Ms. Hannah to West Hollywood Park for the ceremony. They'd set up a podium. Sure enough, Rocky received a medal. A scrum of photographers encircled the boy, shouting, "Look this way, Rocky!" You know, to get his best profile.

Ms. Hannah was in the back row of seats, barking at Rocky, bossing and telling him to get off the stage. After the press scrum left Rocky to cover the rest of the event, our boy realized that he was no longer the center of their attention. Rocky's four big legs busied themselves over to the podium, where he lifted his leg and peed all over it. While the mayor was speaking.

Oh, how I miss my doggies. I've got a stuffed golden retriever looking at me right now.

....

JESSAY'S LTRS ENDED TRAGICALLY

I met the love of my life at church. His name was Don, and he was a short, married minister. I just love short guys. I lusted after Don, but because he was married, and I knew and liked his wife and daughters, we were just very good friends. I would go to his sermons on Sundays to watch him and had to make sure I wasn't drooling on the pew.

Problem was, we had this undeniable connection. I had butterflies anytime we'd be around each other, and if he even came near me, it was like electricity shot through my body. One day, out of the blue, he told me that he was in love with me. I was shocked, more shocked over what he said than he was. "It's okay, I've got it," he reassured me. He was always in control, and that's what I loved most about him.

After having an affair for two years, Don moved his family to Sacramento. I was gutted. He was thinking about his future, and I was living in the present. I was still in Vancouver, Washington, and we continued our affair for a year before I mustered the courage to end it. "I can't do this anymore," I said. The next morning he called me.

"I'm on my way to LA," he said.

"For what?" I asked.

"I quit my church job, and I'm starting my new life."

Don left his wife, and we moved in together in LA. We spent the next seven years of our lives so happy and attached at the hip. I remember a friend invited us to a Super Bowl party. Don and I went down for the weekend, and the joke was that we had our "go steady" clothes on. We would dress alike from head to toe. I worked in a retail store called Jay Jacobs at the time, so I could get two for the price of one, but never in the same color. For example, one of us would wear a red-and-white-striped sweater and the other one would wear a blue-and-white-striped sweater. Clean-cut, tailored. That's what I loved about him. Everything was in order. It was so fun, and it got to where we wouldn't even be in the same room dressing and come out looking alike. Please, girl.

All we did was laugh together. We had such a wonderful life. I was singing, and Don changed careers to corporate insurance. He was always top salesman and won us a Cadillac and trips to Hawaii. Seven years later, I came home after finishing a huge concert in Beverly Hills. I was so hyped. When I walked in the door, he told me he had an incurable disease.

"Give me your credit card," I said.

"What for?"

"Just give me your credit card."

I had to get myself together. I went away for a week, then I came back. "I'm ready to take care of you until you die. I'm committed to us."

It was the hardest year of my life. But what doesn't kill you makes you stronger. And I did get stronger. I couldn't deal with anything but making sure Don was okay. All I did was work and go home. I was up all night long. I'm not sure how I made it through that time without sleep. But I wasn't tired. You just do what you have to do. I had to grow up. I didn't know anything about paying bills. It was very lonely, and, at times, I was so mad at him for dying. But I pushed those emotions out of my head so I could take care of him as best I could. Don passed away on December 12, 1995, at two a.m. I'll never forget that moment for as long as I live.

It took me two years after Don died to even think about dating again. Around 1997, in the very early days of the Internet, I was tooling around online and came across a dating site called Adam4Adam. I met a man named Johnny (not his real name). He had a flattop and a strong jawbone, and I thought he was so sexy. We talked and he was so intelligent. After the day we met, we were never separated again. He moved in with me immediately. I fall in love so easily. I do. What can I say? I'm a serial monogamist.

Johnny and I had intense chemistry. We were together 24/7 for the next ten years. It wasn't like we were hanging all over each other. It was freaky because every time I would turn around, he would be looking at me, and vice versa. We had that thing of just looking back, knowing that you got that soulmate there. I'd never experienced this with anyone, even with Don.

I mean, I loved Don, but this was different. It was a lot more sexual because I was freer. With Don, I was in the straight zone of having sex once a day and maybe on weekends. But with Johnny and me, my God, we were having it three or four times a day. I was letting go. And I was like, *Who are you?* about myself, but I loved me.

Johnny had a couple of red flags when we first met. But he was honest with me about it, and I really appreciated that. He said, "I love you, but I love having sex with multiple people." I said, "Okay," and I was really okay with it because he communicated it, and he gave me the choice. That was fine. Johnny had also informed me, very openly and honestly, that he'd been in prison. It's a long story—a story that is not mine to tell, and it's not the world's business—but he denied any wrongdoing, said he was railroaded, and I believed he was innocent. Fast-forward ten years into our relationship, one day I got a call from his boss. "Johnny is in prison." Same accusation as a decade before. I drove to the jail at four a.m. I put my house up as collateral to bail him out. As we were driving home, I asked him point-blank: "Did you do it?"

Johnny had never lied to me. "I did not."

A jury did not believe him. He was found guilty and has been in prison ever since.

I have visited him in prison, and we still communicate. He calls me about once a month. I told him I loved him, but we can never be lovers again. He can never live with me again because I am not going to have a felon in my house. I'm not going to have parole officers coming into my house at all times of the day and the night.

Johnny will get out of prison in 2028. In the meantime, I still take care of him—I even have a bank account set up for him—and make sure that he's got everything he needs because his family has disowned him. I'm the only person who writes to him. His family hates him. They always hated him even when I was there, and they didn't like me because I stood up for him and wouldn't take it.

I'm very loyal. When I commit, I commit to one person. I don't know how people can do anything else. It takes enough energy with one. This valley's scary. I mean, even the married people are screwing around and I'm the monogamous freak here. I don't know how people can handle more than one person. Also, people don't want to discuss stuff. I'm a talker. Let's communicate. That's the key to relationships, in my humble opinion.

Even though both of my long-term relationships have taken tragic turns, my heart has not hardened. I'm open to finding love again. I'm always looking for another ten years with someone special. I'll be the first to admit it's not easy. Real love is so hard to find. But I'll never stop being in a committed relationship. When I come in, I close the door.

ROBERT GAVE UP ON MONOGAMY

I met my first partner, Mike, in the Art and Architecture Library at Washington University. It was not an overly sexual relationship, but over seven years together we shared many wonderful experiences, including multiple trips to Europe and building a real estate empire. My second relationship began with a chance encounter at a popular park cruising spot in St. Louis and quickly became an intense, combative sexual relationship that consumed both Chris and me for the next nine years. After those two situations, I never lived with a partner ever again. Not in an emotional context.

The last serious relationship I had was in San Francisco in the early '80s. I met Phillip at a bar on one of my many trips to the city before I moved there permanently. We tricked out (aka casual sex), then every time I would come back, we'd get in touch and get together.

After I moved to San Francisco we reconnected, and he and I became very good, close friends. He helped me out in many ways because he was a very bright guy. But at the same time, he was kind of a hippie. He was into music and culturally sophisticated. He worked for one of the big law firms as a word processor and introduced me to the computer in 1981. It was a thrill. He pushed me to get an IBM PC, then he taught me a lot of the fundamentals. Whenever I'd have problems, he would be my go-to for help.

We saw each other romantically weekly. We never lived together, even though I knew he wanted to. I really liked Phillip a lot, but I think Phillip was in love with me. I was not all the way in love with him. I really don't know why I never went to the point of establishing a committed-type relationship. I have some theories.

I had just come off a very nasty breakup with Chris in St. Louis. By the time I got to San Francisco, I had an education in what relationships meant. So my expectations for who I would want to commit my life to were a bit more rigorous than before. Plus, the first year that I was in San Francisco I partied a lot because I had money, and I didn't have a job. I wasn't even looking for a job. I spent all of my time getting to know the city and having a good time. It wasn't until my second year there that I decided, *Okay, it's time to find a job and get to work.* I got hired by the city planning department and immediately became totally engrossed in big projects, like the Giants' new stadium. So I was working eighty-hour weeks.

On top of that, and perhaps most importantly, I think AIDS had a lot to do with my skittishness because so many people were dying around me at the time. At a certain level, I was operating in a way to avoid becoming emotionally attached to somebody who might die soon. It seemed safer to not seek out a committed relationship.

I guess you could say Phillip and I were in a situationship for about ten years, the entire time I was in San Francisco. He would frequently take me out to different musical concerts over at the Greek Theatre in Berkeley and down on the peninsula for music gatherings. I remember seeing Pat Metheny and, on gorgeous Sunday afternoon, a jazz pianist who played on an estate somewhere around Hillsborough in Silicon Valley, high up, overlooking incredible views. Phillip and I sat underneath a big tree, and it was a dreamlike setting. We took several trips together. We went to Yosemite National Park and another time stayed at his parents' house in New Jersey. We went into Manhattan to see Broadway plays and crawled all the gay bars on Christopher Street.

Phillip wouldn't get mad that I wouldn't commit, but he would get sad. We both dated other people, and there was no jealousy. When I moved to the desert in 1990, Phillip came down to visit me several times. We kept our friendship going until the early '90s . . . until he became sick with full-blown AIDS.

I did not go up to San Francisco when Phillip got sick. I was getting regular reports on his health and all. But I very deliberately did not go up to visit him because I knew the emotional toll it would take on me. After having lost so many friends, I couldn't deal with it anymore. By then, there were medical therapies that were starting to come into play. And the epidemic was starting to slow, and everybody wasn't in a panic. But it was still too overwhelming to me. I do have some feelings of guilt that I wasn't there for him in the final few months of his life. Phillip passed away in 1992.

I haven't had a serious relationship since he died. Even though I have no desire to be married, I've always been in the camp of fighting for marriage equality. I just personally never understood why gay people even wanted marriage, a cis-hetero creation that doesn't look all that enjoyable to me anyway. I'm actually glad that I am gay because my relationships are not encumbered by government involvement.

I like my life the way it is. I don't long to have a partner because I don't feel like I need a partner to complete my life. If you find the right person who is truly a soulmate, it's such a wonderful thing. If you are partnered to somebody that after a short period of time evolves into disharmony, it is absolute fucking hell. I've experienced that, too, and I've seen so many other people experience that. I don't want that. I can live a totally happy life by myself.

BILL'S BREAKUP NEARLY DESTROYED HIM

One hot summer afternoon in 1979, I was working at Galleria Design Center in San Francisco when a transformer blew out. There were no lights in the showroom, and it was hot and stuffy. So we closed up shop and I headed to the Castro for a cool, refreshing drink. I sat down at the end of the bar at Twin Peaks, ordered a scotch, and lit up a cigarette. The attractive guy next to me started chatting me up. His name was Bart, and he seemed like a fun guy.

"Hey, you want to go to another bar?" he asked me.

We went to another bar, he ended up coming home with me, and the rest is history.

It's funny because I happened to be seeing another guy, named Art, around the same time that I met Bart, and I couldn't decide who I liked better at first. I left for Puerto Vallarta for the holidays and both Art and Bart got me the exact same Christmas present—a portable cribbage set I could take on my Mexican vacation. When I returned, I was busy with Market Week and put both boys on the back burner. In February, on Valentine's Day, Bart called me up and asked if he could come over. Well, he brought a loaf of French bread, a block of truffle mousse pâté, and a bottle of Dom Perignon.

This guy knew the way to my heart. After that night, we were inseparable for the next sixteen years. Fifteen of those were wonderful, and the last year was hell. In the beginning we were madly in love. Monogamous, and we trusted each other. Bart always had high-profile jobs, which, as we all know by now, I absolutely love. When we first met, he worked at a very popular bar on the pier called the Waterfront. Then I introduced him to a friend of mine in Sausalito who was a sommelier at the Carnelian Room, a white-tableclothed institution fifty-two stories above the city in the Bank of America building, so he went to work for them. After that, he was the editor of *Key* magazine, which was in every hotel room.

Because of that job, Bart was constantly getting things thrown at him. Free tickets to the opera; trips to Hawaii, Paris, and the Douro Valley in Portugal, to see firsthand how port is made. We had carte blanche at all the best restaurants. The biggest thing Bart and I had in common is that we both were foodies before foodies were even a thing. Wherever Bart worked, I had free rein. I could go in anytime and eat. In fact, quite a few times Bart asked me to escort his mother up to the Carnelian Room for Sunday brunch. I would take her up there, and Bart would wait on us hand and foot while we noshed on foie gras and oysters overlooking jaw-dropping views from the Bay Bridge to the Golden Gate Bridge. Bart also had a nice trade account with the landmark Fior d'Italia in the San Remo Hotel. I could go anytime and charge whatever I wanted, even if Bart wasn't there.

Shortly after we met, Bart bought a houseboat on Richardson Bay in Sausalito, and I moved in with him a year later. I hated giving up my beautiful $500-per-month apartment in the city. It had a garage and double Dutch doors leading to the kitchen, which overlooked a lovely garden. But the houseboats were architectural gems dating back to the beatnik era, when artists, writers, and poets set up the colorful community. I wasn't about to pass that up.

Our houseboat was one of four hundred in the Bay, and a mere 360 square feet. It was a converted World War II landing craft and had a diesel engine. The boat could actually drive underwater. We put a roof on it and put a couple skylights up and docked a little nineteen-foot runabout with a 180-power dual rudder motor. We went waterskiing a lot; Bart was really good at it. Or we could take the boat over to Tiburon and park it at one of the restaurants. When the Blue Angels were in town, we took the boat out on the bay and they flew right over us. We'd cruise around the island and wave at all the tourists.

The other neat thing was, all I had to do was walk a mile to a bus stop, which would leave me off in downtown Sausalito. Then I could take a ferry across the bay if I needed to go into the city. When I came back, I'd stop and have a martini in the village before heading home to the houseboat. I had the best of both worlds.

We had a wonderful life together. Until we didn't.

Bart had always been so fun and made light of things. But after fifteen years together, after living in a 360-foot houseboat together, he changed. He was grumpy all the time. I couldn't quite put my finger on what was happening. I remember I pulled his sister, who was a minister, aside at Christmas and asked if she knew what was wrong with Bart. I asked her if she knew a couples counselor, and she gave me a phone number.

At first, Bart did not want to go to counseling. Once we finally sat down, the floodgate opened. We were both a lot to handle when we got in those leather chairs. Things got heated and there was lots of yelling. Lots of stuff was coming up that I didn't even know was an issue. But we were still together. Then I noticed that Bart was going to bars by himself after work a lot. One Saturday morning, he woke up and announced he was going to the Russian River for the weekend by himself. I was stunned. After he left, he forgot something and came back to the houseboat, where I was lying on the sofa sobbing.

"Stop that," he said coldly. Which just made me cry harder. He took off as I was drowning in tears, so confused.

When he returned from his weekend of solitude, he revealed that he was depressed and suicidal. I told him he should do a counseling session by himself. Big mistake. Oops. He came back from therapy with a rehearsed Dear John speech about how he'd been sugarcoating his real feelings: "I've been nonconfrontational until now. I've decided we should break up." He called it a midlife crisis, and that was not the truth. He obviously didn't like me anymore. Bart put a $50,000 price tag on the boat and asked me to give him a $25,000 deposit and he would carry the rest of the loan. (Bart had never wanted to open a joint checking account—keep that red flag in mind in your next relationship.)

I didn't have $25,000, so I called my mom, who loaned me the money the next day. Bart informed me he was buying a condo in Hunter's Point, and needed the deposit for a down payment. All of this happened in a mere five days and then, unannounced, he moved in with his mother in San Rafael. He was very controlling about our breakup. Bart wanted to go around to our friends and tell everyone that we were splitting up, but everything was okay and amicable. I didn't know where I was or what I was doing, and I went along with the whole charade.

The truth was, my head was spinning. I had no idea what happened and to this day, I still have no idea. And he wouldn't tell me anything. It was just over, kaput, and I was expected to move on with zero emotional outbursts? I didn't think so. I had too many questions. Was he cheating on me? I didn't think so but couldn't be sure. In hindsight, I think he was just bored with me and wanted to go out and sow his wild oats. That's the best take I can come up with. The worst part was that Bart was the guy who always gave everyone else love advice. But when it came to our split, he was silent. The lack of transparency, the dearth of answers, drove me mad, literally. After my doctor prescribed the antidepressant Celexa, I developed bipolar disorder and had a nervous breakdown.

My moods were fluctuating constantly. I didn't realize I was changing, but at work they noticed my personality was changing. No one could do their job quite right enough for me. People complained that I was too harsh. They said, "Bill, maybe you need some time off. We'll give you a month of family leave." When I came back from that family leave, I got angry about everything. I started crying and they took me to HR, and I just cried and cried. They made me an appointment at the Langley Porter Psychiatric Hospital in the city. I remember walking in the door and bursting into sobs.

They had me come back the next week to try some medication, and then they kept upping it. So they started with two hundred milligrams. And then I ended up taking five hundred milligrams four times a day. And they wanted me to take it exactly at the specific times of day to calm me down because I was manic. My head was going a million miles an hour, and I was spending money. One of the things that people do when they're bipolar is they spend outrageous amounts of money. And I basically spent about $40,000 in three months. Now, $30,000 of that was a Sebring convertible that I leased. I'd always wanted a convertible.

I realized I didn't want to be around people anymore. So I ran. I moved to the Russian River to Guerneville, which was very gay, and got an apartment there. And I spent most of my time moping around alone. I decided after a year, it was time to come home. The doctors finally took me off my medication and I realized being off it what had happened to me over a very dark eighteen-month period. Eighteen months that were literally taken from my life. I went to a psychiatrist to wean me off these pills that had been making me "crazy," to enable to me to get back into society. I haven't taken any mood-altering medications in twenty-two years.

I can't say that there was a silver lining to the worst time of my life. But I did learn a valuable lesson. I got through it because I wanted to get through it. A lot of people would've just stayed in that same dark place, but I didn't like where I was and crawled my way out of it. I wanted to get back to my happy normal.

Once my moods leveled off, that wasn't the end of my problems. I had all this debt piling up behind me, so I had to file for Chapter 11 bankruptcy. That really affected me in the future because I didn't have any credit. It's hard to start your life over in that situation.

A year after we broke up, Bart met a new partner, Dick. I was a mess at this point, selling dope to make extra money to help pay for the houseboat. I was still trying to stay communicative with Bart. I remember I had to meet my dealer in the city and asked Bart if I could wait at his new place. He said yes because Dick was spending the weekend on their sailboat. Then he got a call from Dick and asked me to leave. "Richard needs to come home and shower, and he doesn't want to see you." I left.

That was in 2004 and was the last time I saw Bart. I'd thought we would live together until the end. That was stability for me. But it blew up in my face. I couldn't accept that someone could just walk away like that with such a flimsy excuse.

In the meantime, it took me years and years to get over our separation. And I was still having money issues. In 2003, I sold the houseboat for about $125,000, and the way it stands it's worth ten times that today. Depressed and lonely, I moved down to the desert that year to start my life over. You know how it is when couples break up: your friends sort of go in different directions. I bought a house in Palm Springs but lost that one in foreclosure, too. Suddenly, I was broke, living on about $1,200 per month in Social Security payments. I didn't have any money at all. I was pinching pennies. I was at the lowest I'd ever been in my life. I was floating through life like a zombie. I didn't go to bars looking for love. I had no desire for sex. In fact, I was abstinent for ten long years. With my mentality, I wasn't that attractive or that much of a catch. I had always enjoyed life up until this point. Now I was down. I was lost.

That's where Robert and Mick came in. Once I reconnected with Robert in 2005 at a movie night at someone's house, my life started back on an upward trajectory. I was in my abstinence phase, so I definitely wasn't interested in their orgies (I honestly had no idea they were going on!), but I'd have dinner with them all the time. Money was tight for them, too, at the time, so we shared what food we could gather up, and that's how we made our first dinner parties.

Bob, Mick, and I became family. Then once the Old Gays became a thing, my confidence came roaring back. I kept reading comments on our TikToks that people thought I was cute. For the first time in years, I felt attractive.

So here we are today. I would like to fall in love again. My biggest regret in life is not having a partner. But I'll take my new three best friends any day. They saved my life.

PART III

Our Second Acts

11
HEALTH

Raise Your Hand If You're Ensure!

"LGBTQ adults face unique stressors—stigma, discrimination, the fear of violence—which can both indirectly and directly lead to disease. The community faces particular, pervasive obstacles that take a toll on the brain and body."

—*NEW YORK TIMES*

The Old Gays have been through the wringer when it comes to physical and mental health—HIV, cancer, autoimmune disease, heartbreak, ya know, the uzsh. But like a vintage Timex, we take a licking and keep on ticking. Today, we've found the best ways to keep our minds and bodies on the straight and narrow, or shall we say gayly forward and fit.

JESSAY HAS HAD TWO LIFE-THREATENING ILLNESSES

In 1998, I came about as close to death as humanly possible. I was working for the California Pacific Methodist Church and performing with the Gay Men's Chorus of Los Angeles. After a weekend concert, I woke up with the whole bottom of my face swollen. I went to a doctor, and he told me it was an ingrown hair. This went on from June to September with this stupid-ass doctor, as I just kept shrinking. I withered away to ninety-seven pounds. It was scary for my friends because they didn't know what to do. And my family had no idea what was going on because I didn't want my mom to know. I didn't want her to lose her child. I just didn't want her to worry. So I managed to avoid seeing her and I didn't tell her.

Apparently, I had gotten MRSA from somewhere. I'd never heard of it. It's a dangerous staph infection that's difficult to treat because it's resistant to antibiotics. You usually get it while at a hospital, but I hadn't been in a hospital. To this day, I still don't know where it came from. Since I didn't know what MRSA was, I never went to a hospital. I was at home dealing with what I had been told was an ingrown hair. But I had a sixth sense that something more serious was going on.

I had just started working at the church and didn't have any sick days, so my boss gave me hers. I'll never forget the kindness she showed to me. I couldn't do any of my singing jobs because I was too embarrassed to be seen in public. My face was full of sores, and I was constantly wearing a mask. This was long before COVID-19 made mask-wearing the norm or even socially acceptable. I looked and felt like an alien, like how people made fun of Michael Jackson for wearing a mask. He was way ahead of his time, as always.

Anyway, that MRSA infection was a fight. I was so beaten down and tired of people asking me, "What's going on?" that I finally gave up. I knew that I was dying, and I made peace with it. I was ready. I remember saying to myself, *This isn't as scary as I thought it would be.*

My coworkers at the church turned out to be my spirit guides and guardian angels. I was sitting in the office one day, barely keeping it together, when my coworker, a good friend who had gotten me the job, walked in. "I'm taking you to a new doctor," he said firmly.

I met with the first female doctor I'd ever visited, and she told me I had MRSA. She said, "Lie down." She started scraping my skin while I lay there crying. "I'm sorry it's hurting," she said sweetly. I thanked her profusely for being proactive. I don't remember her name, but I called her Dr. God. She gave me antibiotics, and the next day it was like nothing had ever happened. Yes, I'd suffered for months needlessly. The moral of this story is, get a damn second opinion!

The MRSA drama was heavy. Yet that was nothing compared to when I started treatment for prostate cancer in 2019, before we all hunkered down for COVID-19 quarantine. I did it alone. I freaked out. I may look like the strongest guy on the outside. Truth is, I hate being by myself. I'm still that way. I'm not a loner. Because my mind wanders and plays tricks on me. I have pity parties. After my diagnosis, I tried to keep myself busy and my mind distracted to prevent my mind from taking me down roads that I'd never gone down and old familiar roads I never wanted to go back to.

When I was first diagnosed a year earlier, they wanted to remove my prostate, but I didn't want to be cut on. I didn't want to do the DaVinci method of drilling five holes in me and sucking everything out. And I don't like chemotherapy. I made an appointment with a new doctor at Loma Linda Hospital, renowned for its proton treatments for cancer.

"Why are you here?" he asked me.

"You know why I'm here," I answered.

"I really don't know why you're here. Have you seen your X-rays?"

"No."

He showed me a teeny little thing we had to strain to see.

"I'm not doing anything. Let's see where this goes."

A year later, we did the proton therapy, a form of radiation. They put you in a body cast, like a coffin formed to your body. Then they shoot radiation directly only to where the cancer is so it doesn't get anywhere else in your body. And they give you a shot with this gel that hurts like hell right in your scrotum. The doctor said, "It's not gonna hurt." And here I am upside down with my butt in the air screaming, "It's burning!" I told him at the end, "If you weren't a handsome man . . ." He and the nurses were just laughing at me.

It was an eight-week journey smack-dab in the middle of the pandemic. I loved the drive, though. I was doing a hundred miles an hour because nobody was on the road. It took an hour to get there and fifteen minutes to get the treatment. It didn't hurt that badly. Being alone was my bigger issue. Previously, I'd been in relationships when I'd gone through stuff. This was the first time I had to tackle something by myself because you couldn't see anybody, of course. All I saw were masked men at the hospital every morning. And they had to cancel the support group, because we couldn't be together. It was rough. But God carried me through it. My doctor made me laugh. And two young people who went to my church worked there and got me early morning appointments. They took care of Jessay during the entire ordeal. They were wonderful.

I gained a lot of weight during this time. I have type 2 diabetes, so I have to watch what I eat. I was sitting at home smoking a lot of pot. I was having some stomach pains related to the treatment, and marijuana helped soothe that and helped me sleep. Unfortunately, it also gave me the munchies. I would laugh sometimes cause of the things I'd put together to eat: green beans with potato chips, and ice cream and cookies and then drink a Coke. Anything that I looked at, I could eat it. I didn't care, I'd eat the green beans raw. I laughed at myself until it wasn't funny anymore. I needed to get the bad stuff out of my house. I love my sugar; I love my carbs. I don't love my vegetables. I can go three months without touching a vegetable.

I remember one night sitting in the middle of my bed with all this junk food around me. My mouth wanted it. My stomach was saying, *Stop, stop, stop.* And I couldn't stop. That was the last time I binged. From then on, I said, "Mm-mm. I don't want nothing to control me." I was miserable, and I couldn't fit into anything. Now I've cut back on my sugar, which is hell, and if I can't sleep, I take a melatonin.

The proton therapy worked. I go every six months for checkups to make sure everything is fine. The only lingering issue from cancer treatment is that it caused some erectile dysfunction. That's a big deal. It's my manhood. People are like, "Man, it's not all about sex."

"You're right," I say, "but that's easy for you to say because you're not going through it. I thought the same thing until I went through it."

I'm getting used to living with ED, and things are slowly happening, but it was a traumatic thing to go through, to not be able to have sex. I just didn't feel like a whole man physically, but I luckily have a couple dates that let me know that I'm okay. I feel pretty good. Mine's a time-healing thing.

I look back on my life and think, *What a journey.* I've been through a lot. But I still get up and I go and I'm thankful to be on this side of the earth. I ain't ready to go just yet. I'm a fire, child. I'm also too nosy to die.

BILL HAD A BREAKUP MELTDOWN

I come from a lineage of good genes. My parents were both slim and in pretty good shape. They didn't drink very much. My dad died in 2001 from Parkinson's disease. He donated his body to science because he had polio as a young man. My mom was very healthy. She only had a cigarette back in the days when she'd have a cocktail. She had five very healthy births. She developed colon cancer, but that was taken care of. She lived a long life until the age of eighty-five, when she had a stroke.

My health has always been excellent, too. With one exception—my nervous breakdown after I split with my partner Bart. By the end of our relationship, we'd both developed a bit of an alcohol problem. We wouldn't really hang out in bars, but when we went to restaurants, we could pack it away. I had a couple of drinks every night alone when I came home from work, while Bart was still out working during the evenings in the hospitality industry.

Bart started going to a bar called the Lone Star, hanging around with the leather daddies. I knew he had to work long hours, but a lot of the time he would just wander into the bar, south of Market. I could tell something was really off with us, and to numb the pain I just drank more. If I woke up in the middle of the night and Bart wasn't home, I'd pour myself a Bombay on the rocks. That was my drink. Then I started drinking before going to work, and eventually that turned into drinking at work. My coworkers knew I was drinking, but they just couldn't figure out where I was doing it. I would hide a bottle downstairs in our warehouse, but they were getting wise to me because I saw something that was moved that shouldn't have been moved down there. So I put a little Post-it on the drawer where I was hiding my booze, so if they opened it, the Post-it dropped down. I figured out that people came in after I left and were watching me.

I was a facilities manager at a telecom company and popular at work. But I was losing it. I got called into the office. "Bill, your drinking is affecting your work," I was told. My bosses told me I had to quit drinking, go to a doctor to make sure my liver wasn't destroyed, and go to a psychologist for counseling. No ifs, ands, or buts. If I didn't, I'd be fired.

And I did it. I stopped drinking cold turkey. I didn't join an AA program because my uncle and my grandfather were both alcoholics and they both stopped cold turkey. I guess I just needed someone to tell me to stop. After I said I would stop drinking, I never had an urge to pick up a drink. Today, I have a drink every now and then. My drink of choice is vodka on the rocks with a splash of ginger ale.

Love can make you cuckoo. I equate the burn of rejection, the burn of being dumped with zero explanation, to me going crazy. If that wouldn't have been happened, if Bart would've just sat down with me and told me what was wrong, I might have coped better. I never got any kind of answer. After my mental breakdown, I had no desire for sex. I would spend the next decade of my life practicing abstinence. The ten-year gap started when I moved into the Tierra del Sol apartments in Cathedral City in 2008 and lasted up until 2018, when the Old Gays started. I know that seems utterly shocking, but I just didn't feel good about myself.

I had lost most of my friends in San Francisco, had my partner literally walk out on me in a five-day period, stopped drinking alcohol, suffered an eighteen-month mental breakdown, and started to live alone for the next twenty-seven years.

I'm in great health now, emotionally and physically. I've had a few surgeries here and there, but that's about it. I honestly can't believe I've lived this long. I had a physical last week, and I aced all my blood work, except my cholesterol was up. It should have been a hundred or lower, and it was like 102. I really wanted to know from the nurse what kind of health she thought I was in. So afterward I asked, "Am I in good or excellent health?" And she said, "Considering the job you have right now, you're in excellent condition!"

MICK HAS LEARNED TO MANAGE HIS PAIN

You'd never know by looking at my muscular physique that I've struggled with major health issues. I've been living with HIV for twenty-two years. The only complication I've had thus far were two bouts of shingles—a condition called Ramsay Hunt syndrome. There were facial eruptions, temporary facial paralysis, inner ear infection, vertigo, and loads of electrical pain. I remember soaking sheet-sized towels in a cold water bath, and wrapping my face and head with the entire towel. Less than thirty minutes later, the towel would be returned to the cold water, hot to the touch.

At age sixty-one, I was diagnosed with an autoimmune condition called chronic inflammatory demyelinating polyneuropathy (CIDP). It is a rare condition but prevalent in families with a history of auto-immune diagnosis like rheumatoid arthritis and type 1 or juvenile-onset diabetes.

In January 2017, my left index finger had gone numb. Soon after that I was no longer able to drive due to spasms in my calves and lack of feeling in my feet. My white blood cells have attacked and de-stroyed the nervous system in all four of my limbs. I've been spared because my skeletal and vascular systems are excellent. I've endured treatments, sweated in training, and worked hard these past six years returning to good shape.

Every day I confront numbness, no feeling, and pain of the electrical kind in my toes, feet, calves, arms, hands, and fingers. I deal with pain every day. I've accepted, or maybe become inured to, it. I've learned how to pace myself. Then there are days when I really do suffer.

The hardest days are when I take off my clothes, bathe, and groom only to put new clothes on. Think of the myriad intricate and tiny movements that your hands, arms, feet, and legs are put through to perform these daily tasks. One test therapists and social workers use to determine if a patient is well enough to function on their own with-out assistance is the ability to perform personal care.

There are days when numbing and stabbing pain, spasms, and cramping can lock my limbs, feet, hands, and especially fingers into wild contortion. It takes me twice as long to dress now. That extends to the many costume changes we make during filming. My OG partners have been very understanding and patient.

I undergo a five-hour infusion of immunoglobulin every two weeks, which keeps me alive. If not for this drug made from blood plasma, the only treatment available to me would be prednisone. My neurolo-gist tells me that prednisone is no longer effective in my case.

Training and nutrition are a big part of keeping my disease in check. I don't know what I'd do if I didn't work out using weights. I've had to draw on muscle memory and regrown muscle to compensate for only, I'd say, 70 percent feeling in my feet and toes, hands, and fingers. Balance is a big issue, too. To see that, all you have to do is look closely at me when watching our dance videos.

ROBERT IS AS HEALTHY AS A HORSE

The biggest medical issue I've ever had is being HIV+, but, knock on wood, my viral load has been undetectable for over seventeen years now. The only other really big thing for the past four years is that I've been chronically anemic. That is one of the indicators of cancer, so my doctor has put me through all kinds of tests: MRIs, several CAT scans, and blood tests. Now I'm seeing an oncologist on a regular basis and a hematologist, who is monitoring my blood. Whenever my red blood cell and hemoglobin drops too low, I get procrit injections under my arm, which stimulates red blood cell growth. They keep looking, but so far they haven't found anything. When I go to the doctor and I get all of these tests, I look at what's off and we talk about it. I know things can start to fall apart as you get older, but I don't feel it!

How the Old Gays Stay Healthy

Dancing

ROBERT: All of this dancing we're doing for these videos is starting to affect how we look and how we feel. Our bodies feel lean and flexible. We have more stamina, especially for the important things, if you know what I mean.

JESSAY: I've lost a little bit of my tummy! I had this bony little body with a belly and now it's starting to go down.

MICK: The most wonderful thing about OG is the dancing. It boosts metabolism while building bone strength. It also gets the blood pumping, so it helps with circulation. Movement taps into the mind-body connection. That is important. Movement keeps the mind occupied and mood uplifted. It challenges you and helps forestall things like dementia and real physical disability. We're talking wheelchair here. This is a job with benefits!

JESSAY: We are staying so active. If I weren't in the Old Gays, I'd be sitting on my butt because I love to watch TV. I'm not a reader. Bill gets so sad, like, "None of y'all like to read!" I don't, unless it's got pictures. All my life, I've always been a visual person. My mom used to tell people, "He's the only person who can tell a Bible story by looking at a picture—better than most adults can tell it!"

BILL: I was doing yoga twice a week, which gave me all the physical activity I needed, but then the Old Gays got so busy that I couldn't make it to yoga anymore. So the dancing literally turned into an exercise class for me. I'm not great at dancing, but I certainly do my best. It's really good for your mental health, too. That's the key to exercise. Finding something that you find fun.

Working Out

MICK: Working out, resistance training, and using weights are an integral part of my life. What I can no longer do is walk in the neighborhood or train on a NordicTrack. The arch in my right foot has collapsed. Now my right leg is shorter than my left. I have to compensate with two braces on my right ankle and foot.

BILL: When I had the breakdown, I struggled to have a good opinion of myself. That's when I started yoga to help me.

Muthah Nature

JESSAY: When I start to feel down, I go outside and look up. The sun is so nice. Even a few seconds to get that vitamin D and, ahhhh, I'm fine.

Talking It Out

JESSAY: Whether with a professional or friends, I've learned as I've gotten older, it's okay to talk about things with people. I was raised up in a Black home where it's, "Be quiet, you don't put your business in the streets. Be strong, you're a man. You don't cry." Oh, girl, I'm so glad those days are over. I tell people, cry as hard as you want to. It is so cleansing. When I go there, I know I need to get it out of my system so I can move on.

Meditation

BOB: I've put a new geodesic dome–type structure in my backyard, which I think is really neat. It cost about $2,000, but I think it's going to be worth it. I have a space for it at the end of my pool. I've carpeted the floor with artificial grass, and I'm going to put fans and speakers in there. I'm going to create for myself a perfect environment that I can go into to do mediation, yoga, and stretching.

Hugs Not Drugs

JESSAY: One morning I woke up and put my foot on the ground and I just flooded. I just cried for three hours. Robert sent a group text asking, "How's everybody doing?" And I just said, "I'm horrible." And he goes, "Do you need me to come over?" And I said yes. I'd never done that. So Robert comes over and is freaking out because he's hearing all this screaming and crying going in my house. When I saw him, I cried, "I don't know what's wrong, please just hug me." I just needed to hug. And when he hugged me, it's like everything went outta me.

Ensure

Yes, truckloads! Robert's fridge is stacked with it.

Find Yourself a Gay Doctor!

MICK: When living in Los Angeles, I had gay male doctors. It allowed for candid and private discussion about health and lifestyle. Here in the desert I've made an exception. Currently my primary care physician is a woman. But she's spent most of her career at San Francisco General Hospital, studying HIV. She listens to me. She knows more than I do. I assume she has seen it all. I follow doctor's orders.

ROBERT: With the political climate and many of the red states leaning so conservatively, it's becoming even more essential to be treated by someone who understands your needs. When I first came to Palm Springs, my medical treatment was through DAP (Desert AIDS Project). The doctors and clientele at DAP are mostly gay. They know about HIV and STDs, always a big issue here in the valley.

MICK: I can't imagine being in a rural community that is not aware of our health issues. Fortunately, there are little communities around the country that are gay friendly, like Key West in Florida or Park City, Utah.

ROBERT: I met a doctor during my sexual forays. He was one of the regular attendees of a little group meeting, shall we say, including several here at the house. After a while, I found out that he was Dr. John Stansell, director of the AIDS ward at San Francisco General. He finally decided to move here and open a practice. And he said to me one day, "I'm opening a practice, would you like to come as a patient?" He became my doctor thereafter. And it was pretty easy to talk about sex with him.

MICK: One of Dr. Stansell's partners was Dr. Tony Mills. A graduate of Duke University School of Medicine and a noted HIV researcher and specialist, he has a large practice in Los Angeles.

Arresting to note that Tony Mills is a former Mr. Leather International. I remember the year that he was crowned Mr. Leather California. That year he was featured on a float at the West Hollywood Pride Parade wearing Wesco boots, red striped leather chaps, harness, black Ray-Bans, and leather cap. I don't recall seeing him with a whip, a flogger maybe.

Mr. Leather California was an in-the-flesh personification of Tom of Finland's dom top leather daddy. Placed on the float's apex, my soon-to-be doctor stood tall, booted feet wide apart, proud to display a hard-on for the entire length of the parade's route. You could hear the roar of cheers for Tony Mills and his proudly demonstrated talent as his float slowly made its way on the two-mile journey down Santa Monica Boulevard on a blue, sun-kissed Sunday.

12
AGING

We're Only Getting Older, Baby

Welcome to the "Old" part in the "Old Gays." This is about aging gracefully . . . or whining about it, whatevs, we've earned that right. Our bodies creak, our hair is thinning or gone, we have deep lines on our faces, and many, ahem, fleshy body parts sag or don't work like they used to. "I wish it were otherwise," Robert muses, "but it's just life. There's literally nothing you can do about it." Jessay, who still struggles with his own body image, tries to put a positive spin on it, as usual. "My mom always said, 'Don't grow up. When you grow up, you get sour, you forget how to laugh.'" Our bodies and faces have changed, but one thing that will never change is our ability to laugh at ourselves—and at our saggy body parts. And at the hair in Robert's ears and nose, which Jessay usually pulls out without asking. Sometimes he'll offer to go get the clippers.

FACING REALITY

MICK: What I notice most are the changes in my face. I certainly don't look young and beyond middle age. I've got extensive lines there and have earned every one of them. Look at me when I'm frowning and I've got the face of an old man. I look like my father, which scares me to no end. There's really not much you can do, except maybe to consider a snip here and tuck there. And just smile like a maniac.

JESSAY: I think my lines have increased because of smiling. It gives me character. I've never thought of myself as that good-looking of a person; I feel like an average joe. And yet I'm grateful for my looks. So I feel like I'm still in the zone. I didn't start out relying on my looks to win any prizes, so I don't have much to mourn with aging. Child, there are days I look in the mirror and go, "Oh my Lord," but then I just laugh about it. I get compliments, too, so that helps me.

BILL: I'm very happy with the way I look, and I feel as young as I ever have. I don't feel old at all. I know I'm in good shape. I don't have too many wrinkles.

JESSAY: When you do Botox, you're poisoning yourself. Also, you have to do it again in like two months. I say, that's too much. I'm seventy. Why do I wanna look like I'm thirty? I don't mind aging. I really don't.

MICK: Usually my eyes are red and it's not from smoking grass. I have chronic dry eyes. I've also got these bags under my eyes. Sometimes it shows up when we're filming. I don't think a lot of people care about that, but I do. I use a retinol serum treatment. I have thought about doing a little bit of a pull because I've got these jowls starting.

THE TOOTH FAIRY

ROBERT: I've had bad teeth most of my life, after growing up in Jonesboro, Arkansas, where our water wasn't fluoridated. Later in life, I was affected by acid reflux. I didn't know for years that GERD was eroding my teeth. Now I'm on a prescription to try to help control that.

But right around the time that John came into our lives, I had been going to the dentist a lot and we discussed what to do about my situation. I asked him if there was a point of no return on trying to keep your teeth repaired. When he said yes, I asked, "Where am I in relation to that?" He said, "You're pretty much there." I made the decision to get rid of them and go to dentures.

Over the course of many months, my dentist pulled out batches of teeth. John really impressed me because not only did he take me to my appointments, he sat there for hours waiting for me. It was a very sweet gesture, even when he'd joke about my gummy appearance. Going to dentures has been a hard adjustment for me for several reasons. I find dentures to be uncomfortable, which is why a lot of the time I don't wear them. Sometimes I only wear my upper dentures because it gives my face better definition. Another thing that I don't like about the upper dentures is the plastic coating on the roof of the mouth. I've learned that so many of your taste sensations come from the contact of food to the roof of your mouth. So I miss out on a lot of the very subtle flavors of food, which is a bummer.

The Old Gays poke fun at me about my teeth issues, but I don't mind. They are laughing with me, not at me. I don't have any embarrassment about dentures because there are so many other people in the same boat. If Clark Gable and Emma Watson can wear dentures, then so can I!

BRAINS FOR BIZNESS

BILL: I'm noticing some things about my brain and memory. I don't want to put too much on my plate in one day. I limit that kind of thing. I strive to stay home on school nights and not accept dinner invitations, because those things can wear you out. I want to be in my prime when I have to be. I feel I've been very lucky.

ROBERT: I find myself forgetting things but nothing serious. It's the little stuff. I've always had a problem remembering names of people. And now that we're meeting so many people, it's a little hard for me to keep up with who's who and all that. But I'm hanging in there. You'll notice it when we're filming, and we're just doing bit-by-bit piecing together of videos. The memorization process for that is a challenge.

To keep my mind sharp, I do both crossword puzzles and sudoku. I've always had a particular fondness for math and numbers, and I've always been good at it. I also play games and cards, like Phase 10, Rollers, and Sequence, with our managers/friends John and Ryan five nights a week.

JESSAY: Now that I'm older I can only deal with one thing at a time. If I start multitasking, I forget what I'm trying to accomplish. I'll walk into a room and have to think for ten minutes before I remember what I walked into the room for. I'm always thinking about something else besides the thing I'm supposed to be thinking about. You take it one step at a time.

MICK: Learning and performing the short dances that we do keeps us pretty sharp. Every Wednesday we livestream on our social media apps—Facebook, Instagram, YouTube, and TikTok. You have to keep your mind together. You can't go blank. I'm also still writing. The act of writing, and thinking of stories, really tests my imagination. I've written a blog on OnlyFans, a serial short story about aliens.

BODS FOR SIN

ROBERT: I know that my body has experienced a certain level of deterioration, and this is something that pisses me off. And it pisses me off because I know without a doubt it's something I have full control over. A lot of why my body has physically deteriorated is because I haven't done, for a number of years now, what I used to do every day, which is work out and exercise, lift weights, do stretching, be active. I've kind of become a lazy-ass turd! It's partially procrastination. I seem to find excuses for not doing it, and I'm trying right now to work myself up to it again.

JESSAY: My chest is a little saggy, but it's coming back in because I'm losing the weight. During my cancer treatment, one of the meds started giving me breasts, and my nipples got really sore. My doctor told me to stop taking it, and now my pecs are coming back into view. I'm working against my tendency to lean forward as I walk. I'm constantly trying to correct my posture.

MICK: I don't look at pictures of myself anymore because I am my own worst judge. We just did this one video where we're dressed up in swimsuits that are hot dogs. I looked at myself and thought, *Oh God.* But then Bob said to me, "Boy, Mick, you really are looking good these days." I'm thinking, *What is he seeing?* I'm trying hard not to judge.

HAIR TODAY, GONE TOMORROW

ROBERT: I initially fought it when my hair started thinning back in the mid-'80s in San Francisco. I immediately sought out treatments.

I was in the first experimental trials of Minoxidil. I visited a specialist downtown every week who spread liquid over my hair with an eyedropper and then he'd peer at my head through a microscope desperately searching for any sign of hair growth. There wasn't any. It was very early in the research. I gave up and never looked into it further.

Interestingly enough, the guy who cut my hair was the one person who made going bald all right for me. He was cutting my hair one day, and he was asking me how I wanted it cut. And I remember him saying, "You know, it's all right if you go bald. A lot of people do it, and a lot of people think it's very sexy." He made me feel more comfortable about it. After that, I stopped with the weird comb-over haircut that wasn't fooling anybody and just started owning my baldness.

Now my advice to people is that balding is a natural process for many of us; it's part of who we are; just accept it. Also, it helps to look at other bald people who you think are sexy for ideas about how to figure out what's best for your sexy bald self.

I must admit these days whenever I see a person, particularly a celebrity, that has an incredible thick head of hair, I will be so jealous. Like Shawn Mendes. That's one of the reasons I think I find him so sexy: it's his hair. But I'm also attracted to a lot of guys who are bald like me. Bruce Willis is an example of celebrities who've accepted it and moved on, and I think that's pretty hot.

JESSAY: It was traumatic when I lost my hair in my late thirties. But it's just a genetic thing. It's like when both grandpas are bald-headed, you've got no chance. I tried a hair system, which was hilarious. It was different than a hairpiece; it was a hair system. It was real human hair, and it cost $2,000. They try to match it to what your hair used to look like. Mine was a brown and curly perm. They cut it and taped it and glued it and put it on, and I could wash it and swim and do anything with it.

I remember after I got it done, I went away for a two-week vacation, and I came back with my hair on. Nobody knew who I was. I would go up and talk to people and they were clueless. It was freaky.

I said, "It changed me that much?" I mean, I'm looking, and I still see me!

There was a lot of upkeep. I had to get my system zhuzhed up every month at their hair salon. I had to take the thing off for maintenance and touch-ups, and they would sew in replacement hair. That's the only time I would take it on and off.

Nine years later, one day I was sitting next to my friend Charles at church, and I noticed his shiny, completely bald head. I thought, *I can do this.* I went home, ripped off my hair system, and threw it in the garbage. I shaved the rest of my hair off and went to a party that night. And that was it.

LIMP BIZKITS

MICK: ED, or erectile dysfunction, is a very common thing. I'm in my sixties, and it's a lot harder, pun intended, because of all I've been through. All I have to say is, "Better living through chemistry."

JESSAY: My ED began with prostate cancer treatment. I had gotten Tri-Mix shots for recreational purposes until the cancer. The first time I couldn't get it up, I was so upset, I really lost it, because after cancer, nothing happened when I had sex. I felt dead inside. I felt so worthless. It took several years, but full function is slowly but surely starting to come back. That feeling of despair still lingers, but thankfully I have some special men in my life who make me feel whole.

ROBERT: I have noticed a slowdown. Fortunately, ever since I've been in the desert, I've had very sex-positive doctors. I am able to openly and freely talk about any sexual issues that occur. There is almost always a way to deal with these issues, ranging from sexually transmitted diseases to ED. As a result, whenever I notice a slowdown, I talk about it, and I get a remedy. Now I take Viagra—it's only a third of a full dose, but just taking that little bit daily, I am able to perform almost all the time.

BILL: I remember when Viagra first came out. Everyone was so excited about it.

ROBERT: Now the big thing is Tri-Mix. It's an injection into the penis. I've tried it a few times, and boy, does it work. One time I asked a couple of muscle guys from San Diego I had met to pose naked for me for a sculpture I wanted to do. Unknown to me, they brought some with them, and when we finished our posing session they asked me if I wanted to do some and play for a while. Being a game player, I agreed, one of them injected the dose into my penis, and I quickly developed a hard-on that lasted for hours. After they left, I still hadn't gotten enough sex, so I spent the rest of the day cruising websites and tricking with others who were on the prowl.

MICK: Oh, Tri-Mix is fun. You inject a dose it into the base of your penis. It works in about twenty minutes. Tri-Mix can keep you going for several hours. Years ago when I lived in Los Angeles I met up with a guy. We did Tri-Mix. For some reason mine wasn't taking, so he gave me a second dose. I ended up with priapism the whole next day. I was out of food and had to shop. There I was at Gelson's in West Hollywood trying to cover up my hard dick. I met a cute guy in produce. They say when that happens, you're supposed to go to the hospital. But I said, *Fuck it, I'm going out on a date.*

13
MODERN LOVE

Who's Your Zaddy?

One recent random evening, Mick was standing in the kitchen making himself something to eat, not wearing much clothing—no shirt, compression pants, leg brace—when there was a knock at the door. Mick opened it and standing before him was an attractive young Latino man, about thirty.

"Hi," said the young man.

"Hi," Mick responded.

He asked Mick some questions, but Mick was confused. "I'm sorry, I don't understand."

The young man then showed his smartphone to Mick. It displayed a profile from a dating app. "I met you on Scruff," he said to Mick. "Are you Stryker*?"

---

* Online handle has been changed to protect the not-so-innocent.

Looking at the displayed profile, Mick smiled mischievously, or maybe Machiavellian, and replied, "Oooooh, now I understand! Come along with me."

Mick led the young man down the hallway of the house.

The young man stopped halfway and said nervously, "You don't look like your picture."

"I'm not Stryker."

"You're not Stryker?" the young man replied, his voice increasingly panicked.

"Hey, Bob!" Mick walked to the end of the hall and opened a door.

"Yessss?" Bob answered, his voice tinged with embarrassment.

"Your guest is here!" Mick replied triumphantly.

The young man scurried past Mick into Robert's bungalow.

"I told him to come to the back gate," Robert later told Mick. With a sigh, he added, "Every once in a while, they don't listen."

Yes, Robert may have reached eighty years, but he's still getting some. In fact, all of us Old Gays can still get it. You're well aware by now that we've had, let's just say, oodles of hookups. We have about 240 years of dating experience among us. We feel like we've gathered together solid advice on everything from wooing to one-night stands.

Some may snipe, "Wait, why are you single?" It's mostly by choice. Jessay is in a long-distance romance with a Canadian, Bill has a friends-with-benefits situationship happening, Mick invites a fella he meets online to Spencer's Restaurant in Palm Springs for dinner here and there, and Robert says he couldn't care less whether he has a steady thing. "I feel like there's a part of me that would love to have someone by my side, but I know what a responsibility that is. I'm not sure I have the time or the patience."

We sat down to talk about our thoughts on modern dating. Nothing was off-limits because that's how we roll. You can call this the Old Gays Dating Dossier, if you like. As witchy TikTok tarot readers may reply, "Take what resonates." That is, scroll on and turn the page if it doesn't pertain to you. But it probably will, because love is the universal language!

IS DATING HARDER NOW OR WHEN YOU WERE YOUNGER?

BILL: I think dating is harder now because you don't get to see the person. Before, when I was coming out, I could walk into a bar, look around, and see people, talk to them. You'd find out instantly if you were interested and vice versa. And you didn't have to worry that maybe it wasn't who you thought it was. Now, with apps, there's another little layer in between you and the person where things can get lost.

MICK: As far as relationships are concerned, I don't think a bar is a great place by which to develop a long-term relationship. I met Joel when I was working at a store. He came in and bought some clothes from me and then took me out for coffee. I think it is much harder today. And it can be more lethal, if that's possible. I need to know what I may be getting myself into.

ROBERT: I find it easier. First of all, you're working with some presumably known information. You have visuals; you have stats. They may be off, but at least it gives you entree as to what you can ask in the way of follow-up questions. You don't make a contact unless you are conversing with someone. I always assume the stats are more or less accurate. Probably off by about 5 to 10 percent. At least I know the ballpark. For me it has really facilitated meeting people. I don't like bars. I don't like small talk.

BILL: I think there's something really changed from when we were doing dating—if that's the word we're using. It's sort of the reverse of our early experience. These days kids go to a bar to socialize and then they go home and they get on the Internet to meet someone. Bars aren't really the pickup places that they used to be.

MICK: After coming out, when I was younger, a date meant dinner, usually a movie, and then sex. Now it's just hookup sex. Nobody does dinner anymore. I avoid the bars. Too many drunks and dicey persons.

ROBERT: Maybe we need to redefine "dating." The world has changed so much.

MICK: I remember watching Saturday-morning cartoons with my older sister. There was a popular board game always being advertised called Mystery Date. After a roll of the dice, a player gets to open one of two doors. Behind one door was a picture of a clean-shaven, handsome twentysomething dressed in a tuxedo, holding a corsage. You know, "the dream date." The other dates were the same handsome guy but with scruff, carrying tools, wearing a dirt-covered shirt and overalls. He was "the dud," but to me "the dud" was more desirable.

WHY DO YOUNGER MEN LOVE THE OLD GAYS?

ROBERT: I have had people who claim to be eighteen years old approach me for sex, more than once. I steer away from them. I can just see one of them being underage, and then I'm in a world of trouble.

MICK: We should have a stack of nondisclosure agreements at the front door. The interest among people who are literally less than half my age is what astounds me.

BILL: When I go online I specify an age range of thirty-five to fifty-five, and still half of my responses are kids. I don't even respond.

MICK: The younger generation has a whole different idea about age.

BILL: I've asked guys who really like older guys what it's about. Were your parents married? Did they get a divorce? Most of the time I find that it's the lack of a father figure in their past that carries over to their interest in older men.

MICK: See, I didn't find that. Of the men that I've met, it didn't matter one way or the other. Perhaps it's a fetish. I have met a fair number of youngsters into bodybuilders over fifty.

ROBERT: I've been catfished a few times. It's mainly a much older version of their pictures.

BILL: And out of shape.

JESSAY: They're probably the honest ones. It's the ones who have the pictures of themselves at forty and when you meet 'em they're like eighty. If they're a fake, I just walk. I don't even waste time to say hi. Especially when they say the same thing all the time. They've got the same line. "I'm looking for love only." Oh, please. No, you're not.

WHAT IS THE BEST DATING APP FOR GAY MEN?

JESSAY: Adam4Adam, Scruff, Grindr. That's enough.

BILL: I'm only on Adam. Adam's been around for a long time and still going well. To me, it's the default of a dating site because they had the most advanced features and they keep adding things. Grindr has a hook to it. It's basically GPS. If you walk into a bar and you have your cell phone and you're on Grindr, it will tell you who else is in the room.

JESSAY: I like Scruff and Grindr. They show the people who are close to you.

MICK: I haven't been on Scruff since the first of the year. When I lived in Los Angeles, I usually used BBRT, which stands for BareBack Round Trip.

ROBERT: BBRT is the only one I'm on. I joined it many years ago, and it's more out of habit. I'm aware of Scruff and Grindr, but I just never made the effort.

JESSAY: My friends have been trying to get me on that, but I just don't have a life now.

MICK: I'm not cruising sites. This job and my health, staying fit, are more important than dating apps. Now, if I had more free time, I might pursue that again.

ROBERT: There are quite a few of these hookup sites that are specifically for older gentlemen to meet younger gentlemen. Daddyhunt is one. Rent Boy. SilverDaddies. Back in the '90s, in my wilder days, I did a bit of modeling, and I appeared on several of these older sites as one of their models. And I got paid for it. Once I got an email from a site I never heard of congratulating me for being picked as the model of the month.

ROBERT: Mick says that he hasn't been on many sites lately, but I can tell you that every time we go to New York, he does use his apps. And Jessay does on cruise ships.

JESSAY: Yeah. I do. I've gotten lucky with cruise ship entertainers three times. They find me. I'll be on my dating apps looking to see who's nearby, and ding! They have to be very careful, though, because they're not supposed to fraternize with the guests. I sneak them into my stateroom about one o'clock in the morning. I've never sung with any of them, but we did make beautiful music together, if you know what I mean.

MICK: When I do use an app, there is no guarantee something will come of it. I've had guys who come in and if within a minute, I figured that this wasn't going to go anywhere, I would just pack them up and send them off, saying, "I'm sorry, this isn't working for me."

WHAT'S YOUR GO-TO PICKUP SPOT TO GET LUCKY?

JESSAY: Cruise ships!

MICK: When I lived in West Hollywood, it was the Pavilions grocery store at Santa Monica and Robertson Boulevards. It used to be a Safeway. In *Tales of the City*, Armistead Maupin wrote about "Safeway Social." The San Francisco place to visit, shop around, and pick up a guy in the late afternoon before dinner. Well, we had that in West Hollywood, too.

At Pavilions you'd do the "Safeway Social." The added fun was that celebrities shopped there. I used to see the Australian actress Coral Browne and her husband Vincent Price. One time we, Joel and I overheard Coral purring to her famous husband, saying, "Oh, Vinnie! The lamb chops look *really good* today."

There in the meat section stood Vincent, hunched over and holding a roast in one hand. In the other hand he'd clutched a monocle, holding it close to the meat wrapped in clear plastic. The icon of Edgar Allan Poe horror leaned over farther, bringing the monocle close to one eye. Then back to the bloodred-dyed piece of plastic-wrapped meat, examining it over again and again.

BILL: I have twenty copies of Vincent Price's cookbook. I collected them. Three of them are signed. But it's funny you mentioned Safeway because the same thing was true in San Francisco. The Safeway on Market Street near the Mint was where all the gay guys went. And the Safeway down in the Marina was where all the straight people went.

ROBERT: I can't think of any other place other than online. But as far as just simply meeting and interacting with other gay men, it's on the streets in our neighborhood here. People who are walking their dogs.

BILL: The only place I'd say is that if I wanted to find a husband, I'd go camp right outside Trader Joe's. Actually, that's where I get recognized the most.

MICK: When I lived in West Hollywood, my apartment was right next to the side entrance that had a big metal gate. One early morning, about eight a.m., I was going to walk to Gelson's over on Kings Road. And right in the corner by the door two guys were making out. And they were really hot and bothered because that street was known for cruising.

BILL: I just moved into a new mobile home park. I'm still meeting people. It's a small world and there are a lot of gay folks there. A guy I had dinner with in Puerto Vallarta once, he lives there also. I get invited to so many things. I've been invited to birthday parties, cocktail parties, going-away parties, you name it. I joined the LGBTQ+ group and we play cards and dice games. It's a lot of cliques and heavy on the gossip. But the funny thing is that the guy who's been running the group just resigned because some of the queens complained that there were too many straight people at our events. He was like, "Forget it, I'm out." That's what made the whole thing fun!

WHAT IS YOUR POLICY ON SENDING NUDES?

JESSAY: Nudes. I have no problem. But I need a face.

ROBERT: Yeah, I do it. Don't hesitate.

BILL: I have a face pic, and if someone is interested enough, and if I'm interested in someone, I will send a dick pic.

MICK: My life's an open book.

WHAT'S THE BIGGEST RED FLAG THAT'S A DEAL-BREAKER?

ALL: Drugs.

ROBERT: P and P. Party and play. That means coke and meth. Heavy drugs.

MICK: "Wild fun" and "no strings." Because "wild" and "fun" means meth. And "no strings" means every kind of action imaginable.

ROBERT: Sometimes people's profile title or storyline will include words that will include a capitalized letter *T*. When they emphasize the *T*, it means they're into meth.

MICK: I'm older and hopefully wiser. I didn't try meth when I was in my relationship. But I certainly did experiment afterward. That's why I've said dating can be lethal. You realize, and very quickly, that hooking up is not always about the sex. It can be about the drugs. If

you have feelings of self-love and self-worth, and if you've got it together, there's no place for party.

JESSAY: I remember once I invited a friend over and he brought another guy, who spent too much time in the bathroom. The door was
cracked, so I took a peek, and all of a sudden I just see the guy shooting up. Oh God. I tell my friend, "We're done. He just shot himself
up." I don't know what people are like with that stuff. He got upset. I
just stood taller. My voice went lower. I said, "Fucker, get out of here."
I was scared.

MICK: I know people who have overdosed. It's very sad. Because ad-
diction to methamphetamine can happen with the first dose. With the
right chemistry, you can be hooked instantly. Someone told me that
if you're HIV+, the risk of becoming hooked on methamphetamine is
much greater because of the receptors found on the virus. In the desert you must be careful—it's meth central here. By the semitruck load,
it is brought across the border.

JESSAY: Another red flag is when people ask me for money. I just say
good luck. And jealousy, I don't do that at all.

MICK: Jealousy can be fun.

BILL: I had a roommate who hit on me the first night he moved in.
He said, "There's something about you. Let's go to bed." So I jumped
in bed with him. It was fun. And he brought tricks home, but then he
got so jealous of the people that I brought home that I had to ask him
to move. I'm not proud of this at all. It was really embarrassing. I had
no idea that this kind of thing would even happen. I mean, we were
just buddies hanging around.

MICK: Which brings up Rule Number One: Don't fuck your roommates. Don't fuck your friends, and don't fuck the friends of your

friends. Bob and I are the only permissible exception to the room-mate rule.

ROBERT: It's hard to avoid. When I first moved down here to the desert, it was in the middle of summer, and it didn't seem like there was anyone around. You get a little desperate. It gets to the point where friends are having sex with friends because there's no other choice.

MICK: The cool thing about living in a resort community is that during the winter you fuck the tourists. In the summer you fuck the neighbors.

ROBERT: I have met a few people in just hookups who within a very short period of time I picked up that they were very controlling. And I found it very uncomfortable. Control is something that only comes out over an extended period of time.

BILL: It's a turnoff to me because they are trying to take, and I want something equal.

MICK: In general, people who have control issues mean that their lives are out of control.

BILL: I have always had an arm's-length policy. You go to bed and that's fine, but if they start getting too close to me, that's when the door slams.

ROBERT: And I'm the same way. If I feel someone wants to get closer to me, I push 'em away.

JESSAY: I disagree. I fall in love. But I've learned to keep love out of it. But I love being in the love mode. And I want to stay that way for the rest of my life. It helps that I've learned to communicate more. So I'll say, *Oh, okay, this is what it is,* so I can deal with it without having outsized expectations. But I still prefer it to be about that one man. Even so, some people do cling too hard. I can shut it down quick.

MICK: "Cloying" is the word.

WHAT IF YOUR DATE IS RUDE TO THE SERVER?

ROBERT: I find a polite way to shut 'em down and push away.

BILL: I've been in the service industry all my life, and that is a major red flag.

JESSAY: Unless the waiter is a bitch. I've had that happen where the server was being rude to other people at the table.

MICK: I'll finish dinner with the guy, but I don't think we'll be seeing each other again.

HOW ABOUT TALKING ABOUT THEIR EX CONSTANTLY?

ROBERT: It's okay if they talk a little bit, but if that's all the conversation is about, that's too much. Get away. It's like you're a fill-in.

BILL: They're clinging to something from their past, and that bothers me.

MICK: I don't mind that. Again, I'll listen to it during dinner, and especially if he's paying, I'm not going to walk out on him.

WHO PAYS FOR DINNER IN GAY RELATIONSHIPS?

JESSAY: Do you pay for dinner if you didn't invite someone out?

BILL: That's one of the first boundaries I would set up.

MICK: If I've asked a man out to go to dinner with me, yes, I'm paying. I've treated people to dinner.

BILL: I can't remember the last time I went out to dinner with a guy on a date.

MICK: It doesn't happen much anymore.

ROBERT: I'm the same way. It's been years.

JESSAY: I don't have problems meeting people to date. I'm out there. But I'm not having sex with everybody.

ROBERT: I think a throuple is an interesting concept. I would be willing.

BILL: A throuple sounds great. I was turned off by an octouple once . . . When I was living in Los Gatos there was an English teacher at San Jose State who had seven men living with him. One was an attorney, one managed a market, one was a schoolteacher, etc., and they all pooled all their money together. I got my friend a design job to do the house. One time, I was invited for dinner, and they wanted me to get into the group. I was so shocked because we sat down at dinner, and two of the guys came out in waiter outfits, white shirt, black tie, white jacket, and served us. The leader told another one,

"Donald, fuck the rug." And the kid got down and started humping the rug. It was such a weird situation. I declined the invitation to be part of that group.

MICK: Sounds like a cult.

DO YOU THINK IT'S POSSIBLE TO BE IN LOVE WITH TWO PEOPLE AT THE SAME TIME?

ALL: Yes. Yes. Yes. Yes.

WOULD YOU RATHER BE DUMPED OR BE THE DUMPER?

JESSAY: I hate being hurt.

MICK: Being the only one in the room who's been divorced, it's not a good situation either way. I choose doing the dumping. I've learned to take control of myself. It's sad when a relationship has reached the end. If you want to change that, I think the best way is to reason with the person and say, "I don't think this is working out and here's why." That gives the other person an opening, to respond and say, "Well, I believe this, too," and then you part equally.

If he says, "I would like to stay and here's why. Let's see if we can work it out," should it become clear that the differences are irreconcilable or that there are issues that can only be brought out and worked on in therapy, then I'd rather we end it. Life is too long, even at this advanced age, to put oneself through a meat grinder.

ROBERT: Yeah, for my own self. I'd rather do the dumping.

BILL: Well, that's what happened to me. Because Bart seemed so unhappy with me. I said, "Do you want to split up? Do you want to break up?" He said, "No, no." But he was lying.

MICK: That's the mark of a person who likes to pull hooks out of fish.

HAVE YOU EVER GHOSTED OR BEEN GHOSTED?

BILL: The only sort of semi-relationship I had was with a guy named Otto. He was from Germany. Big guy, very handsome. He did Porsche rallies around the country. Last year I said goodbye to him, because I was going to Puerto Vallarta. When I came back, I sent him a message like, "Hey, I'm back, give me a call." Never heard from him again. Lasted a month.

MICK: I have been ghosted, and I've ghosted other people. Sometimes it's just out of sight, out of mind. I get wrapped up in another project or something and dating is not a big priority for me. I know I've been ghosted. You know, you forgive him. They obviously wanted to move on and you have to as well.

ROBERT: I've done it and been a victim. It's infrequent. I think it's part of today's dating culture. It doesn't bother me either way.

14

NEVER
SAY
DIE

For Real,
Don't. It Hits
a Little Too
Close.

We're still here, we're still queer . . . but we're nearing our
expiration date!

One commenter on TikTok asked about the Old
Gays, "Can't they just die already?" As you've read, we've survived
through extremely tough times. We thought the best parts of our
lives were over. But we never gave up. We never stopped learning and
trying new things. Robert still makes art every chance he gets and
is involved in community government. It's been fifteen years since

Mick's divorce, and he has created a stable, thriving life. Bill volunteers at the senior center. Jessay is the busiest of the group, his dance card bursting at the seams with singing gigs and social engagements.

Still, we are aware that there are two certainties in life—death and Cher. Taxes, too. But that's such an ick. We'd be lying if we said we don't think about death. We do. We just don't dwell on it. We're too busy living. Regardless, here are our deepest thoughts on climbing the golden staircase to that gay bar in the sky. As Harry Styles says, "You can't bribe the door on your way to the sky," but a good BJ never hurts!

BILL BELIEVES IN HEAVEN

Do you believe that the souls of your loved ones who have passed are around you?

Yeah, I do. And especially when some really good things happen. Every once in a while I'll just be sitting there and I'll just say, "Hi, Mom," and I know she's listening. When I'm going up to a traffic light and I make it through I say, "Thank you, Mom. Thank you, Dad." It's just a weird little thing. But I think someone's looking out after me. I get signs they are around me, even if sometimes those signs can be very strange and uncomfortable. I believe that when I've had times of need, there have been people there, not virtually, but cosmically there, egging me on. I've never been to a psychic to connect with them, though, because I already have a personal relationship and a direct line.

Are you afraid of dying?

I'm not afraid of dying because I thought I would've been dead a long time ago. From when I was growing up and the wild lifestyle I've had since. Like anyone else, I would love to die in my sleep.

What do you think happens when we die?

I do believe in God. It's not something I've taken to extremes, but I do believe I'm going to go to heaven and will have a nice time. I was brought up as a Presbyterian. My brother and I would go to Bible studies during the summer. Our parents would drive us down to the church and we'd go to Sunday school and then they would return at ten o'clock and we'd all go into the sanctuary together as a family and pray. So I believe I'm going to go to heaven. I've done some bad things, but I feel I've turned it around, with my volunteering work and giving back in ways that I can. My sister is a big believer that we're all gonna meet together in heaven. We talk about seeing our brother, our sister, our mom, and our dad, and what a glorious occasion it's going to be.

What do you think the afterlife looks like?

I have a very happy view of the afterlife, so that makes it less fearful. We'll be floating on big white clouds. And I've already heard the music that will be playing, and it's like an organ with deep bass tones. It's glorious. Everybody is happy and smiling. I believe there is a tangible God in heaven. It's not someone or something that comes up in a cloud of smoke. Most of my belief in God comes from the church's art and music. The love and devotion that went into the paintings and sculptures created by man are a testament to the glory of God. I am a big fan of requiems and church hymns.

If you got hit by a bus tomorrow, is there anything you didn't do in life that you wish you had done?

No. I've had a very complete life. My only regret is signing off on all those houses to get the hell out of my relationships!

What kind of funeral would you like to have?

A dinner party thrown by my closest friends with the most fabulous food, wine, and music. Just please don't sing "Candle in the Wind."

JESSAY BELIEVES GOD IS GOOD

Do you believe that the souls of your loved ones who have passed are around you?

I talk to my mom constantly, but I don't want to hear her talking to me. I believe the dead know nothing, you know? The spirits are there, but it is my game that I play, that I lean on her. I talk to her daily, thanking her and telling her how much I miss her. And I wish I could have done more for her. I don't feel that I didn't do enough for her, but I wanted to do more because she did everything she could for us. I love her. And my sisters, I just wanna hug 'em all the time like I did. We were very, very close. I feel for families who don't have it.

I miss my siblings and my mom so much because we were all in this thing called life together and it was nice to have that family closeness. All of a sudden, it was like everybody was gone and I'm still dealing with that. Mom passed away ten years in March. Losing my two younger sisters was really hard because both of them just dropped dead. Each was found by their kids. My one sister died in the bathroom getting ready for work at the university where she taught. My second sister, I had just talked to about her crab cakes the day before. She was going to send me some. So she ate her crab cakes, and then she was dead that day. I said she died with my crab cakes! Those women were my life.

I haven't gotten any signs, though. My BFF does. She says she's been around ghosts, and I tell her, "That's for white people. 'Cause Black people ain't putting up with that shit."

Are you afraid of dying?

Well, I've been close to it once, baby, when I had MRSA. It was a very calming journey, the journey to death. I felt that I was going to die, but I was so at peace. And it surprised me. I said, "Child, aren't you scared to die?" Evidently not. I was not scared of death.

**What do you think happens when we die? And what
does the afterlife look like to you?**

I don't know. I've got no idea. I feel that my spirit is going to go
back to where it came from. My body is gone, and it's gonna be
cremated, so it can't do much. I believe in the second coming of
Christ, even though I sometimes have my doubts. It's like, okay,
we've been talking about this for years. I'm seventy now. I have a
friend, she's 110. She's watched her children die before her. I don't
know that part of it. I just don't know. I just have to believe. When
I doubt, I get out of my head. I just believe that God is good. And I
don't try to talk anybody else into it, because we're all on our own
journeys. As for an afterlife: child, I have no clue. I don't even think
about it.

**If you got hit by a bus tomorrow, is there anything you
didn't do in life that you wish you had done?**

I really want to travel more. All I want to do now is go on cruises. I
want to see the world. I would like to be able to buy a home. I don't
know if I ever will be able to again. I had a home, and I just got tired.
It was financially draining. And it was like a new roof, sump pump,
windows, doors, it was constant upkeep.

Honestly, I'm just so thankful to be here, because evidently, I had
the Old Gays to come together with. Everything brought me to where
I am now, the journey to Palm Springs. I tell people, "Can you believe
a little colored boy from Greeneville, Tennessee, is living in Palm
Springs?" I thought it was all white and millionaires. Then I found
out it was cheap to live here. I have never felt so at home since I left
my hometown.

What kind of funeral would you like to have?

Now, why should I have a party for everyone but myself? I'm gonna
live my life to the fullest until I can't anymore—so my funeral party
is the party I'm having right now.

MICK ALREADY EXPERIENCED LIFE AFTER DEATH

Do you believe that the souls of your loved ones who have passed are around you?
Only our beloved dogs.

Are you afraid of dying?
I don't fear death. According to Bob, I've died three times, at least. In 2019, two years after I was diagnosed with CIDP, I became depressed. I was taken off immunoglobulin due to complications, and it was ineffective. The disease continued to advance. Meanwhile I had dropped the dosage of prednisone that I was taking too far and too fast. I locked myself in my room and stopped eating. I collapsed. Bob called an ambulance, and I was taken to the ER at Eisenhower Health Center. There, they put me back on immunoglobulin. Because I'd fallen, I was subsequently placed in a nursing home. Three weeks later, after I had returned home, I had a seizure. I crashed into the master bedroom mirrored closet wall and slammed my face onto the exposed concrete floor.

Bob found me bleeding and immediately called another ambulance. This time I was taken to the trauma center at Desert Regional, where they kept me for eleven days. Bob was told that had he found me an hour later, I would have died. I had significant injuries to my left eye and socket.

After surgery to remove a piece of wood that had punctured my left eye, and additional days in the ICU, I was sent back to the same nursing home. This time, the staff assumed I wasn't going to live. After I beat that assumption, they said I'd never walk again. I was given a wheelchair. The doctor on duty, however, said, "Nuts to that." A nursing assistant took away the wheelchair and gave me a walker. "If you want to go to the bathroom, you walk," he ordered. I did. After one hundred days, I left convalescent care.

The third time was during COVID-19 quarantine. On May 11, 2020, I overdosed on gabapentin. As the ambulance was again taking me to the trauma center at Desert Regional, the paramedics sliced my throat and were ready to attach me to a ventilator. At the same time that was happening, I, still very much unconscious, saw myself in deep space, hanging with both hands from a bent lateral row bar. Two white strobe lights illuminated me. I heard a voice, not male or female, say, "Look, you can come with me now, or there is still time to go back." I remember not saying, but thinking, *Yes, I want to go back. There's something I have left to do. There's something that I need to finish.*

Evidently, I'd started breathing on my own. My sister, who was tracking the ambulance online, said it was traveling up Sunrise toward Desert Regional. All of a sudden, the ambulance turned right onto Ramon Road and headed to Eisenhower Health Center.

I was put into an induced coma briefly. When I woke, they transferred me from ICU to the hospital. where I recovered for nine days. I was placed on what is called a 5150 hold. Whether intentional or not, this was considered a suicide attempt. By law they were required to hold me for three days to undergo a psychological evaluation. I remember thinking to myself, *You mean I came back for this?*

Finally, I was discharged on May 22, my sixty-fourth birthday. I returned home through the back door, nervous about how I was going to be greeted. The first person I saw was Robert. I was met with open arms from him and my entire Old Gays family. It warms my heart, even though I looked like death warmed over. In fact, if you look at a video we made around that time for Pride, a Diana Ross number, you can see that I'm using a walker.

I do not dwell on those years of struggles. I reflect on my brief interaction with what is considered to be existential or simply profound. I choose to continue with life. I live from moment to moment because living with an autoimmune disease and HIV means every day is a new adventure. That means living with dehydration, fatigue, headaches, muscle cramps and spasms, and nerve pain, and taking fifteen prescriptions a day, not including supplements like extra salt.

There isn't time to indulge myself with self-pity. Instead, I challenge myself to reach a new level of fitness in the weight room. I follow the advice of my older sister, who has lived with rheumatoid arthritis since her early twenties. She is retired now after years working full-time as a prosecutor. She told me, "Every morning I give myself thirty minutes to feel sorry for my fate. Then I spend another half hour in meditation. I shower, get dressed, feed the dog, and get on with my life."

What do you think happens when we die?
We meet our destiny.

What do you think the afterlife looks like?
Black space punctuated by shafts of white light.

If you got hit by a bus tomorrow, is there anything you didn't do in life that you wish you had done?
None.

What kind of funeral would you like to have?
There will be no memorial.

ROBERT BELIEVES IN THE MYSTERIES OF THE UNIVERSE

Do you believe that the souls of your loved ones who have passed are around you?
My experiences with a few close friends who've died and being in a hospital room with them and seeing and feeling certain things happen. I do think there is something there, but I don't for the life of me know what that is.

Are you afraid of dying?

I do not have any fear about dying, mainly because I reached eighty years old, which is a long life in anybody's book. And the life that I have lived is a good life. I have nothing whatsoever to be ashamed of. Were I to leave this earth today, I'd go knowing I've done all that I could ever have dreamed about. I'm satisfied. And because of that, I don't fear dying.

What do you think happens when we die?

I don't believe there's a good place and a bad place that you go to. I don't believe in heaven or hell. I do believe a transformation that takes place. I don't feel at all bad that I don't understand it. Science is proving that out. How can we be the only ones in this vastness?

What do you think the afterlife looks like?

Spiritually, I think about the universe and the expansiveness of the universe, and I see the results coming back from the various space telescopes as more and more discoveries are being made about the universe. It's such an enormous concept that I don't feel like I have a clear understanding of what happens once I am no longer a conscious person, but I do think there's something mystical that happens. I've had too many experiences in my life that reinforce this. You know, I go back to the incident I told you about earlier with the bird. I genuinely believe it was a messenger. It was that bird that got me through that very dark period in the years immediately following my bankruptcy and the battle over my house. I feel that I was told that everything was going to be just fine. I think I've gotten those kinds of messages at various times in my life—when I needed them—but I didn't pay as much attention to them as I did then.

If you got hit by a bus tomorrow, is there anything you didn't do in life that you wish you had done?

I can't think of anything I regretted doing or that I still have on my bucket list. I feel good about the life I've lived and if that bus hit me tomorrow, I feel complete.

This is not to say that there aren't some things I wished I'd done differently, and I welcome whatever experiences are ahead as a further expansion of a life well lived.

What kind of funeral would you like to have?

I don't want any big funeral or anything like that. Just a simple little get-together by a few of my chosen family. More important to me is, when I reach a point where I am physically or mentally impaired to the point I can't function, I want to die in this house. That's something I want to write into the legal documents. I do not want to go and sit in a nursing home to be among a group of people who are dying. I wanna be in my home when I die.

I used to want to be cremated, but now I'm starting to think a little bit differently about it. I'm hearing a lot about how people are starting to think of their bodies as organic material and as being a potential component of the earth. There are places that specialize in this process of drying out the body and putting it through a process where it becomes fertilizer so we go back into the earth to provide nutrition for what comes next. So, whether I'm incinerated or I become compost, I want my remains to be spread on the grounds of my house.

15

TIKTOK STARDOM

Make Your Work Your Passion

So many of our fans write us and say, "I felt so terrible today. I didn't want to get out of bed until I saw you on TikTok. I laughed. For a few minutes, I forgot about my situation in life." These words send our hearts soaring! It's far better than fame any day! Countless numbers of our fans thank us for our dance videos, irreverent humor, and message of love.

We're not going to lie, however, since having become a TikTok phenom, the experience is an absolute blast . . . absolutely! Here's the behind-the-scenes story of the creation of the Old Gays. All your burning questions will be answered here. But if that burning doesn't stop within two to three days, you may want to call your doctor!

THE CHEMISTRY

ROBERT: My tenant John was really the first one to pick up on this chemistry we had going. He would join our dinner parties and observe our interactions. He thought that they were humorous and interesting. When he started dating Ryan, within the first two months he lived here, they both thought something special was there.

OUR FIRST SHOOTS

ROBERT: The first filming was just three of us, and we weren't paid anything. It was just a lark. There was no budget, aside from rideshare transportation to LA. We weren't being driven to LA yet in limousines. Ryan drove. They were extremely long days, between shooting and the back-and-forth from the desert.

BILL: We were bootstrapping at that time. None of us really had any money or were making very much money.

MICK: I'll never forget the time we filmed our first brand partnership that we had gotten from *RuPaul's Drag Race*. I was at death's door in the hospital but got out just in time to make it to the shoot.

BILL: By our second shoot, Robert had picked up Jessay across the street and asked him to join us. The second thing Ryan wanted to do was throw us in drag. So he took us to a bar named Trunks, which sadly closed recently, but they used to have a drag night every Friday. Ryan brought in a dresser, a makeup artist, a soundman, and a video guy. I remember waiting in the back room at Trunks. I didn't know what to do. I was being so demure, but all I remember about the night is when we got on the stage, Jessay got up there and just threw his arms up and flew around the joint like he owned it. Fabric was flying everywhere.

ROBERT: He'd done this before. The place was packed. We had to walk out to the end of a twenty-five-foot runway. The crowd did not go wild. They clapped. I don't know if I'd call it enthusiastic. It was more like, *Who are these clowns?*

BILL: Robert had a nickname and everything for his part.

ROBERT: I looked like Phyllis Diller with a big blond wig. You do kind of adopt the personality of what you're wearing.

MICK: Drag is performance. You're playing a character. Drag artists don't look anything like the characters they've created. It's a way for people who may be naturally shy to express themselves. A drag artist creates a unique character that may be completely opposite of what they believe themselves to be. Drag can open the door to explore deeper issues. Watch Dame Edna and you will see how she comments on celebrity and fame. It's satire that can be tough medicine yet it's wrapped tightly around the sweetness of humor.

BILL: I remember when I got into drag, all of a sudden, my voice went very, very demure.

MICK: You fought it tooth and nail. I remember you didn't want to do it.

BILL: I was the only one who had to wear three-inch spiked heels. I was so nervous. They had Jell-O shooters going around all the way. I didn't dare touch one.

JESSAY: You were scared you were going to fall flat on your face. But once you got the dress and the hair on, honey, you were just floating.

BILL: They gave us $200 each.

ROBERT: That was a big payday.

MICK: I must have spent that pretty fast.

THE MOMENT WE KNEW

MICK: We did a TikTok video dance to the song "Good Day." Ryan shot it in one take, like the famous *Goodfellas* scene.

STRENGTHS AND STRUGGLES

MICK: Looking back on it, we've advanced so much since then. It didn't work out well the first time. After that first time, we came back and did it a second time. Because we had a little extra time to process it, we rehearsed it again, and it flowed. It was beautiful. And then the response. That's when it felt like lightning in a bottle. Viewership shot up from that one. That's when we finally gelled as a group and we knew that we could work together. We had the confidence now, knowing that we may not get it the first time, but if we rehearse it, even if we come back to it the next day, we're going to be better at it.

From my perspective, Jessay is the only other person other than myself that has had professional experience. Bill and Bob are not trained performers. They have been immersed in this endeavor with very little training. They take direction pretty good. Bob and Bill have answered the call and have responded with aplomb and vigor. I hope they understand the value of their contribution.

JESSAY: I'm surprised I can dance as well as I do because I can't balance on my left foot anymore. I've had surgery on my feet twice. Ryan doesn't have time or patience to teach the moves anymore, so he will record himself doing our dance moves, send the video to me, then I teach the rest of the guys. Sometimes individually, sometimes as a group. Robert just goes with it, but Bill has the hardest time with choreography. He's a spoiled little rich kid, and you have to hold his hand because sometimes he will be shaking. But he always gets it. He has it sometimes and doesn't realize that he's got it. I say, "Why are you being so hard on yourself?"

MICK: Part of it is learning how to let go and just do it.

JESSAY: One thing we all struggle with is dips. We can drop it, but then we can't get back up.

MICK: Once you understand how a piece of choreography flows together and tells a story, you just give in to it and fly.

JESSAY: I don't like to talk. I have a hard time memorizing lines. Everybody else starts saying their lines and I lose it. That's my hardest thing.

ROBERT: For major lines and deliveries, we rely on Mick, 'cause he has the training. He also seems to have a better memory than we do.

MICK: Memorization is part understanding how individual lines or lyrics flow together to tell a story. That's how I'm trained. You want to be in the moment, total immersion. It's all about staying in that moment. Moving from line to line, beat to beat, and leading to a resolution or conclusion. It's harder than people think to perfect, you know, to establish and maintain focus or concentration. That's what my fellow OGs are learning.

JESSAY: The proud mom.

MICK: I have to work on patience. Sometimes I know it's going to take, quite frankly, twice as long to get something done because I'm not working with professionals here. So I save the best for last only when the camera's running. Because I only have so much energy.

JESSAY: As I say, memorization for me, I freak out. On the outside I'm looking fine. But on the inside, a lot of times I'm on the verge of tears. But I will not let them come out.

ROBERT: But when he does it, he does it well.

MICK: I want to walk up to Jessay and say, "Hey, relax, you've got it. You just have to let go." You know, it's like that old adage about wanting to go pet a dog. If your mother grabs your hand and says, "No, the dog will bite," once you lay that into a person's mind, you're always going to think the dog will bite when you go to pet the dog. And what does the dog do? Bites you. It's a self-fulfilling prophecy.

JESSAY: Bill memorizes everything.

BILL: I do have a pretty good memory. Sometimes it's hardest depending on how it's worded. It can be really difficult to get it to flow off your tongue. But I type out my parts and highlight them and everything.

MICK: Bill can't always bring it forward. I see him tense up and he forgets . . . because of stress, I think.

ROBERT: The more dancing we do, I feel more and more relaxed. I'm not going to say it comes faster, but when it does come, I am now getting into the part more than I did at first.

MICK: Bill and Robert sell themselves short. We are doing far more complex moves than we did even with "Good Day." When I look back at "Good Day" now, I believe that choreography was easy when compared to the work we're attempting nowadays.

JESSAY: I always say, y'all don't know what went on during this. I learned about myself that music lyrics don't mean shit to me when I'm trying to get the choreography down. I'm a beat person.

BILL: You and Mick are both beat people.

ROBERT: Jessay is the first go-to for a dance move.

JESSAY: I'm always out front, not by choice, honey. Mick's out front a lot and he can't even walk.

ROBERT: There's frequently a discussion as to who's going to be in front because the lousy dancers go in the back.

MICK: Ryan has put Robert up front.

ROBERT: I'm there by default.

JESSAY: I love being in the back, too, but I don't get a chance that much. Bill tells us where we're going.

MICK: Actually, that's Jessay. You're always giving orders.

JESSAY: I've got more power.

ROBERT: We talk about it as a group. That's one of the biggest changes. Ryan used to do all of the creative and then bring it to us and tell us more precisely. What we do now more and more is have brainstorming sessions about the videos. We develop our lines, who says what, and dance moves. We do that very well.

MICK: We work out the lines. Decide who is going to do what. Then we put ourselves in costume, or whatever works. And we shoot the video. Lately the brilliant thing has been that we can shoot things out of sequence. Everyone understands how it flows together. We have really good continuity. It shows in our latest videos. We are working as professionals who remain authentic.

GROUP CONFLICTS

ROBERT: When we work together, we work well, but we don't always work together.

MICK: Last Wednesday was a horrible day. Ryan called it a day. There was no creativity from any of us. Then yesterday, on Thursday, we had one of the best sessions we've had all year.

JESSAY: Yes, yesterday we had a ball. Time just flew by.

ROBERT: Issues that come up are environmental, whether it's too cold or hot for us to film and how to compensate for that.

BILL: Not only us, but the camera itself. It overheats. And Ryan has to stand there with an umbrella, shielding the smartphone.

BILL: But we realized something productive yesterday. Ryan wanted to do live sessions just to loosen us up and get us ready. It really works. So now sometimes we play a game for the first half hour just to loosen us up.

JESSAY: I like to jump in and do that. I'm all about getting the dust up so I can get it out.

ROBERT: You know, it is like a marriage in a sense.

MICK: Oh, without a doubt it's like a marriage. With no bling and no sex, thank God.

JESSAY: Except for that time you and Robert hooked up.

MICK: It's like being in a band. What's the difference between the Rolling Stones and the Beatles? The Beatles were like fire on water, and soon they flamed out. They had different creative visions. John and Paul went in different directions musically. When I watched the documentary about the *Abbey Road* album recording sessions, it was George Harrison who walked out. It was not over John or Yoko. George fumed at Paul's self-promoting behavior.

JESSAY: Which Beatle are you?

MICK: Robert Reeves wouldn't let me go. That's why I'm stuck here. You have to make the best of it. And no one's weeping for me.

BILL: Three-day notice.

MICK: That's what Bill always says when he wants to shut me up.

OUR FAVORITE OG MOMENTS

BILL: We did a Shake Shack commercial for Pride in 2021, and we met a politician there, an assemblyman from Orange County, who asked us if he could take his picture with us and made it his Pride picture.

MICK: I love when people greet us at airports or events. There's a lot of goodwill.

BILL: Another favorite moment was the maiden voyage of the *Discovery Princess* cruise. We stopped in Cabo, Mazatlán, and Puerto Vallarta in Mexico. That was my first cruise. Everything was free. I mean, strawberries and Veuve Clicquot champagne. The whole banana. It wasn't a gay cruise. It was almost like a soft opening for the ship. All the bartenders were Croatian, and they didn't know how to make a drink.

MICK: I got violently ill the first night out on the cruise. I'd eaten fish for lunch. We were in the French restaurant having a lovely time at dinner. Suddenly, I excused myself, rushed to a bathroom, shut the door, and thought I'd locked it. I'm bending over the toilet, holding the rim with two outstretched arms, heaving my guts out, and somebody opens the door on me. I managed to chase the person out. After locking the door for sure this time, I overheard this person shout out, "Hey, there's a guy in there heaving his guts out! On the first night!!!"

ROBERT: I didn't go. I was sick.

MICK: I was convinced to venture out on the third day. Jessay and Bill have a favorite spot in Puerto Vallarta: the Green Chairs on Ritmos Beach. I arrived for lunch, finding Bill, Jessay, and Ryan camped out there. Ryan was so sweet, he arranged for a private car to pick me up and drive me to where these fellows were enjoying themselves ogling the hot men. The cruising was decent for March.

ROBERT: Another time that's memorable was when we went to New York for *The Drew Barrymore Show*. We stopped in four airports there and back, and in every airport people would recognize us and want to have selfies taken. When we got back, we said, "Hey, a lot of people know who we are!"

BILL: When we went to Las Vegas, we'd been out to see the *Magic Mike* live show. As we were coming back into the casino, this tall, beautiful young lady wearing a slinky dress with spaghetti straps screamed, "Oh my God!" She ran up to Bob and planted a kiss right on his lips.

ROBERT: There were a whole bunch of college girls screaming in the lobby of the hotel.

MICK: I remember that Ms. Slinky Dress was drunk. When she screamed, that was the first time a reaction freaked me out. We aren't exactly Harry Styles.

ROBERT: The rest of them didn't hear what she said. But when she came up to me, almost nose to nose, she said, "You're my favorite."

JESSAY: I have one story. I wasn't with the guys, but I was at a bar called QUADZ. This guy from Orange County came up to me all excited. Fine, fine, fine, fine, fine, hug him. He came back to me again, and shouted, "OMG, OMG." I'm like, *This is getting too much.* And he just kept doing this. And I finally said, "You're making me uncomfortable; you're drawing too much attention to me and I don't like it. Can you leave?"

BILL: We really haven't been out in public that much as a group, but when we are it's quite the spectacle. The one time that we were out in public by ourselves was when we were invited to the Soho House for Coachella, and we were mobbed. First of all, they put us in a little gazebo and had an interview with us. Then it took almost an hour to get where we were supposed to because people were everywhere.

This was the deal we did with Hugo Boss. They dressed us up in our outfits. On Friday afternoon they put us in a red Jeep, and we drove all around Palm Springs waving at people. On Saturday, we went to Coachella.

ROBERT: Straight guys love us, too. I think there is clear evidence that the younger generation doesn't care.

MICK: It's an altogether different generation, and it's so wonderful to watch. They are our fan base. They get and are hip to LGBTQ+ issues, people, and rights.

BILL: I'd say twenty- to thirty-year-old females.

MICK: Half of them live outside the country. We receive comments from people everywhere in the world, from Finland to China to Brazil.

ROBERT: I'm definitely conscious about it.

JESSAY: I'm boring, so I don't have to be conscious. I hug a hell of a lot more and I love it. If someone nicely approaches me, I say, "Now that you know who I am you gotta come up for a hug."

BILL: One of the biggest joys is going out and being recognized. It happens every time I go to Trader Joe's or Target. People seem so heartfelt, and it's a joy to be seen and to receive so much warmth and enthusiasm.

JESSAY: On Friday nights I get mobbed at QUADZ. It's a video bar, but it's all the old show tunes. Everybody asks, "Where are the other guys?" I tell them: "They're in bed. And not with each other." Sometimes people assume we are hooking up with each other. I've had people ask, "Have you guys ever had sex together?" I go, "Hell no." And they say, "Well, I want to come have sex with all of you."

I go, "Well, that ain't happening. We're family, and it's not incest here."

BILL: I used to go to the bars every once in a while, but now I'm nervous to go out alone.

THE BIGGEST PERK OF BEING AN OG

ROBERT: We've gotten lots of clothes. Many of which we wouldn't wear out because they show a lot of skin.

MICK: People love to see skin.

JESSAY: Many I don't wear 'cause it's polyester.

BILL: Rihanna sends us underwear from her Savage X Fenty collection.

FAVORITE CELEB COLLABS

BILL: One of the most exciting things we've ever done was walking the red carpet at *80 for Brady*. We met Jane Fonda, Lily Tomlin, Rita Moreno, and Sally Field.

MICK: We were in the press line sandwiched between *Access Hollywood* and *Paramount Social*. *Access Hollywood* didn't like us being there. They complained to me that we were encroaching on their space. I guess because we weren't really press.

BILL: The nicest person there at the opening was Tom Brady.

MICK: Tom Brady is the GOAT of American football. Yet, he walked up to us and *he* started the conversation. Totally accessible and modest. A mensch. I was tongue-tied.

MICK: Bill did meet one of his idols. He always wanted to meet Jane Fonda.

JESSAY: My favorite celebrity collaboration was with Paula Abdul.

ROBERT: We did shoot at a TikTok collab house with her and armed guards.

BILL: These kids were paying $80,000 a month to live in the house.

ROBERT: There were probably thirty or forty very young people there.

BILL: It was very contemporary. Now, Drew Barrymore. She's the real thing.

ROBERT: She was our first real celebrity that we got to meet. And she was so nice to us.

JESSAY: Down on her knees during commercials talking to us. Then she'd go back to her chair to shoot.

MICK: Yeah, she was very passionate.

ROBERT: The person I would like to become a good friend of is Billy Porter. We met him at *80 for Brady*. We told him who we were, and he freaked out and said his husband had sent us some suits and swimsuits to wear for a TikTok, which we did. He said, "We'll catch up more in Palm Springs." I sure hope so!

MICK: Michael Bublé was nice. We got the chance to meet the Jonas Brothers. It was a pleasure to meet Nick Jonas, because I think he is a rising star and his own individual.

BILL: There is something about Nick Jonas. Ryan had thrown out a question once, like, "Okay, who's your favorite guy right now?" And I said, "Oh, Nick Jonas." So when I met him, I said, "I mentioned you." And he said, "I know!"

JESSAY: I can't believe Bill's not saying Gus Kenworthy.

BILL: He came up and gave me the biggest hug when we were on the red carpet at the *80 for Brady* premiere.

MICK: Did he smell good?

JESSAY: He wouldn't let us near him. He was already U-Hauling him away for himself.

BILL: Because we were flirting with one another when we did a video once. He was right next to me, and within the first five minutes, I gave him a kiss.

JESSAY: I remember Jane Fonda coming up to us and she was like, "Who is this?" She looked half scared.

MICK: Jane didn't know who we were but said, "I think I should know who you are." Lily Tomlin was being Lily. Sally Field didn't know who we were. Ryan explained to Sally, "We're on social media." A bespectacled Sally crinkled her face into a frown and said to no one in particular, "I hate social media. I'm never on it."

JESSAY: Okay, girl.

BILL: But Mick drew her in, too. He asked Sally to choose between baseball or football. And they immediately had a conversation.

FUTURE GOALS FOR THE OGS

BILL: For me, it would be being number one on the *New York Times* Best Sellers list. Also, I would like to get out more and be with our fans.

JESSAY: I want to go to every Pride parade.

ROBERT: We would make great motivational speakers. The best thing about a Q&A is there's no script. You're speaking from the heart.

MICK: We want to bridge the generational divide between LGBTQ+ youth and seniors. I think we're onto something here. You see a cycle working. We are nourished by our fans and we nourish them back. It's important to give each other hugs and support. We're a minority in this world. We must band together and stay focused on what's really important. It's not about survival anymore. It's about taking our rightful place in the world.

Mo' Money, Less Problems

There are so many people out there who worry that they won't have enough money for retirement. Most of the Old Gays have experienced major ups and downs with money, so here are the biggest mistakes we've made along the way and our best advice to be able to retire in comfort but still have fun.

Bill: "Don't give up your property without a fight."

I wasn't that good with my personal finances. I made it by, but I didn't have big dreams of being a millionaire or anything like that. That to me was just way, way out there. I lost everything a couple of times, and I regret and take responsibility for my actions. I gave away three houses to my ex-partners, simply because I wanted out of the relationships and couldn't deal. The lesson is, deal with it. It's too much money to just give away because you can't handle drama. I could have made it hard on any one of those individuals, but at the time money didn't matter to me. Money should matter to you, at any age. You must plan for your future.

I bought my first house with John in Laguna Beach, but when he started acting erratically, I wanted out of Dodge, so I signed a quitclaim deed. I made the same mistake with Michael, the trust-fund baby from Chicago. In the mid-'60s, we bought a beautiful house together in Los Gatos on a third of an acre for $45,000. It was a one-hundred-year-old Victorian and had every kind of fruit tree in the yard. It even had one of those brass-cage elevators that went from the ground floor to the second story. When Michael and I split, he said, "You didn't put any money into this place, so I would like you to sign a quitclaim deed." I had contributed money and labor to bring the Victorian house up to par. I'd paid half the mortgage and was responsible for converting the old coach house into an income-producing rental unit. But I did it again and signed the quitclaim deed.

Then the houseboat debacle happened. When I moved to Palm Springs in 2003, I bought another house and threw all my money into it, then lost it in the 2008 Great Recession. I don't even know if my family knows about these things. I guess they do now. I was so broke I did my grocery shopping at the dollar store. I always made a list so I didn't buy unnecessary things. I always made sure I wasn't stoned when I went shopping. Those are the small things I did to keep myself afloat.

Robert: "Don't overextend yourself."

When I entered the business world, one of the things I learned through observation was the theory of OPM, use other people's money to build wealth. Borrow if you have the opportunity. That's how I built up my real estate empire. We would get these big chunks of money that we would use to reinvest and acquire more property. I had made so much money I was able to pay cash for my first house in San Francisco and spent almost $200,000 on its renovation and addition.

I started having financial issues once my business partners and I made the decision to gradually sell off our assets. Then I was diagnosed with HIV. As I mentioned earlier, I moved to the desert and lived like there was no tomorrow because I thought I might die. I was spending profusely on dinners and going out. By the '90s, when I felt I was in the last years of my life, any thought of building for the future just totally disappeared, and the attitude was enjoy it now, while you can. Around 1992 that moment hit when I came to the realization that I wasn't going to die and I better get my ass in gear and start making money again. I didn't want to lose my house, so I got back to work, selling art and working as a landscaper at adults-only resorts. My brother loaned me $10,000 here, $20,000 there, and that made it possible for me to survive until I got back on my feet. There was definitely a time when I was scared I wouldn't be able to support myself, and I spent a lot of time actively thinking, *What am I gonna do?*

The biggest lesson I learned was that I spent money in an unproductive way, whereas earlier in my life, I was very conscious about trying to spend money in ways that I felt would grow over time. I think that's the key.

Jessay: "Surround yourself with smarter people."

I've always struggled with money, but I've never given up. Once again, it's the prayer thing. All I know is, it's kept me strong at so many rough moments. There were times I didn't know how I was going to make some payments, but it always happened. I put it out into the universe, and I had no problems. I would ask to borrow money from friends, but I paid it back. I had a rule with myself: if you can't pay it back, don't borrow.

I was blessed to have some friends that could help me out. I try to do same thing for people, be there for them because I know what it's like to not have and to suffer. I have gifted things because I know some people could never pay it back, because I know what it's like. And I try to do my best and to be fair. But don't take advantage of me. I know who my friends are. I won't give acquaintances a penny. Well, I will give 'em a penny. I just helped an acquaintance the other day because he was having a hard time. I don't want people to suffer. But I'm careful. I know it could be here today and gone tomorrow.

My late partner Don took care of me financially. He paid the bills, and he spoiled me. When he got sick, my eyes were opened. All of a sudden I had to grow up. I got angrier and angrier at him for making me grow up. I had to take a deep breath and say, *Okay, you're responsible now, so this is what you gotta do at forty.*

Today, I make sure to fill my world with people who are smarter than me. I'm smart enough to know that I'm a commoner and I don't know a lot of stuff. That's why, since the Old Gays, I have a financial advisor. I listen to my advisor. A good leader puts people around them that can guide them through things they know nothing about.

Mick: "Save, save, save."

The Old Gays was a godsend for me. That's because when I got sick with CIDP, it was right after I had a hip replacement. Between the copay on my hip replacement surgery and now not being able to work, I'd completely depleted my savings.

I did finance things through credit cards and lived on them for a while. Try and stay away from that if it's possible. Credit is a good thing, but not to an excess. I did the food banks. I did SNAP. I did all that stuff. All I had was my Social Security Disability payment, and that doesn't go very far. The entire situation, not to mention future, was dismal.

I fully expected to be working until I was age seventy. I thought, *As long as I am healthy, I can continue to work.* Well, coming down with an autoimmune disease destroyed that. The process of getting qualified for Social Security Disability and actually receiving a benefit payment takes five months. Next, I had to wait twenty-four additional months before I qualified for Medicare.

A large part of my decline and subsequent hospitalization and convalescence is due, I think, to being taken off a PPO and assigned to Medicaid. The Medi-Cal provider I'd been assigned refused to pay for immunoglobulin treatments. The only reason why I was able to get back on a limited dosage of immunoglobulin was because I ended up in the emergency room.

I know it's hard to make ends meet these days, but try to save money. You never know what the future holds, especially when it comes to your health. I wish I had been more prepared.

16

HAPPINESS

It's Your Choice

The OGs answer one of life's most often asked questions: What makes you happy?

ROBERT: I think one's definition of happiness definitely changes over time with different phases of your life. But I know for me that the times that I feel most content, which I equate with happiness, is when I feel like everything I need to address is addressed and I've done a good job. And that I don't feel like there's anything I have to do. When there is no stress, then I feel more content, and therefore I feel happier. I think there's a day-to-day happiness and then there's big-picture happiness. The big-picture happiness is connected to the direction of your life at that phase of your life. Are you happy with where you live? Are you happy with what you're doing? All of those are part of the big picture. And then the day-to-day really comes down to what level of stress you have. Are you battling it now? Maybe this is just today. If you ask me tomorrow, my definition of happiness might change.

MICK: Only Americans talk about happiness. In the Declaration of Independence, we are guaranteed "the pursuit of happiness." With that as the premise, I choose to paraphrase Marlene Dietrich, who said, "I do not think we have a right to happiness. If happiness happens, say thanks."

I'm right in the middle. If you think of all the goals and objectives that you've pursued throughout life, you know that you'll never reach perfection. That's not why we're here. I don't think the goal is happiness. For me, my goal is to experience life in all its diversity and humanity in all of its strangeness. I have a great curiosity. I would say, if you want to pursue something that feels like happiness, then that's fine, but you have to define what that is. Really, what is *your* happiness?

BILL: Weed! To me, marijuana is so good. Because it takes you away from where you are into a better place.

MICK: Recreational drug use is pervasive within our community. Some of that is pure escapism. Like the Madonna song "Vogue." If you listen to the lyrics, especially in the verse, she talks about all the things that are terrible in life. But the one place you can go is to the dance floor. Let yourself go. Vogue. In so many ways, that sums up the gay experience.

JESSAY: I find joy in my music. My rehearsing takes me away, but it slaps me in the face sometimes. And I laugh at myself.

MICK: Since I turned age fifteen, the one constant that I've had in life has been my training. It eliminates stress. I'm so focused. I'm in the moment. My heart rate is up; blood is pumping through my system. For those forty-five minutes, my cares really do evaporate.

BILL: I feel that way about food. I am in the process of writing a cookbook based on my mother's collection of three-by-five recipe cards. I collect old menus from restaurants that I admire and/or have visited. In 1989 I rented an apartment in Paris for a month as it was the two hundredth anniversary of the storming of the Bastille. My partner came to visit me for a week, followed by my mother for another week. I had never been to a three-star restaurant, so before leaving for France I wrote to Taillevent asking for a lunch reservation. We had lamb prepared three ways, foie gras mousse, and sauteed shrimp. I wish I could remember what we had for dessert—I'm certain it was chocolatey and decadent—but it was the grandest meal that I ever had. I took French in high school, and I went to Alliance Française for a crash course in French. I ordered our lunches speaking French and was very proud of myself. At the end of the meal the waiter brought out the dessert menus and I again ordered in French. The waiter then spoke to me in English and said, "Monsieur, I must say that your French has improved greatly since you drank that bottle of wine." We all laughed, and then the waiter brought us snifters of Cognac, and that ended one of the most perfect meals I have ever had.

MICK: Bob is the happiest when he's working on the house. The whole house is his work of art, his creation, everything you see.

ROBERT: My spa went out of working order sometime around 2016. I was still struggling with maintaining financial stability, so there was this period of time from around 2016 until now where I couldn't use it. And people who came over would make fun of it. "When are you going to get the spa working, Bob?" and all. But the fact was, I couldn't afford to do anything about it until I received the money I've made with the Old Gays. Now I have capital again, and I'm able to pay these big bills. Last night, after I got out of sitting in the spa, I was walking back to my room and Mick was up watching television. I turned to him and I said, "I finally feel like my life is whole again."

BILL: Love makes me feel whole. The happiest I've ever been is when I've met someone who I really like, and they really like me. And all of a sudden, the world is a different place. I joke about how I love falling in love with love. It's intoxicating. That's the ultimate happiness. But I love being alone, too. Happiness, to me, can be quality time with Bill where I can just sit back, relax, and just really enjoy myself and not worry and not think about anything at all. Also, happiness to me is a good book.

JESSAY: My secret to happiness is not allowing anybody to make or break my day. I depend on me. And try to spread the joy. Only you have control over your joy. I got upset a few weeks ago at something and for three days I had a headache. But the anger was at myself for allowing something to take me there. I don't like to go there.

My biggest time of happiness is when I am not working and I'm actually getting to hang out with friends. That just makes my day, laughing and catching up. Another thing that makes me happy is right here in my heart. I talk to my mom a lot. I know she's no longer with us and she's not going to talk back, but it helps me. We were really close, and while she's been dead eleven years, she lives on brightly, right here in my heart.

ROBERT: Find something you love to do with your life and be the best that you can be at it. Look within yourself to understand and know who you are. And then be who you are.

BILL: I've had a passion for every job I've had. I've loved everything I've done. And that is the greatest happiness in the world. I feel badly for people who are unhappy with their work. I want to say, *Then move already!* but I know it's not always so simple and it can be scary to change, even what you don't like. To that I would encourage everyone to find the courage to change what they can and if they can't change their situation, to try to change their experience of it.

ROBERT: I don't think a lot of people really grasp how much control they have over their lives and how powerful they can be if they simply harness what's within them. And you've heard it from different people: half the job is just showing up. And if you decide you want to change the system, all you have to do is show up at some meeting, start speaking your mind, and you're going to find yourself moving up in that world, and you can become a truly powerful person.

Epilogue

Our lives used to be about sex, drugs, and rock and roll. Now it's about *Magic Mike* movies, prescription Rx, and smooth jazz. We have lived queer history, from the darkness of the closet to light that shines so brightly today. When you've been around the block as many times and for as long as the Old Gays have, experienced all the triumphs and tribulations, and weathered more ups and downs than Stormy Daniels, it's impossible not to learn a little something along the way. We hope our stories have inspired, helped, and comforted you, or at the very least made you laugh and/or gasp in horror.

Before we started the Old Gays, things were looking a little grim for Robert, Jessay, Bill, and our boy Mick. We were heading into our twilight years with our eyes glazed over, on autopilot, honestly. None of us had a clue that something so monumental and earth-shattering would strike us like lightning and give us a renewed zest for life. Listen, you don't have to become a TikTok star and walk down the street in a couture gown with your junk on full display to change your day-to-day from drab to fab.

Are our lives perfect now? Of course not. Robert just fell and bumped his head. Mick can't lift as much as he used to. Bill is still searching for that unconditional love. And Jessay misses his mama. Not every day can be sunshine and rainbows (though we come pretty close to that living in the desert). We've doled out a lot of advice here, but unfortunately, we don't know the secret to finding happiness. Because happiness 100 percent of the time is impossible. Over our lifetimes, we have learned to tweak our expectations and, in doing so, are the happiest we've ever been.

We just want you to know that, wherever you are on your own journey, life can turn on a dime, if you're open to trying new things and just saying yes to opportunities that fall into your lap.

Bye, gays!

Acknowledgments

The Old Gays would like to thank:

Ryan Yezak and John Bates. Without them there would be no Old Gays.

Ryan, for his hard work, dedication, perseverance, inspiration, and unparalleled creative abilities—not to mention his astounding ability to wrangle cats.

Our brilliant editor, Karen Rinaldi at HarperCollins, who really understood our mission and believed in us and encouraged us to delve deep. She's a good egg.

Our very supportive agents, Rebecca Rusheen and David Doerrer at A3 Artists Agency.

Our butchy collaborator, Dibs Baer, who was able to take three complicated lives, plus one simple queen's existence, and turn it into a seamless story.

Jessay would like to personally thank: My mom, Mrs. Jannie Martin, who was a saint and still lives in my heart. My sisters, Jacqueline Carter and Aubrey Della Shoemaker, who just let me be me. The Palm Springs Gay Men's Chorus and my church, the Glendale City Seventh -day Adventist Church, for being my safe haven. It's not just a church; it's a family. And my amazing Old Gays, my fellas, who invited me into this world and are forever wrapping their arms around me, even when they don't know they are.

Bill would like to personally thank: My mother, who was my best friend and supported me in any way that she could. She was totally nonjudgmental and one of the kindest people I've ever met. My brother, Jim; sister, Julie; and their spouses, for their continued support of me throughout the ups and downs in my life. My extended family for always having a positive outlook. And to my Old Gays family for loving me even though I'm a lousy dancer.

Robert would like to personally thank: My chosen family, who have been with me through the ups and downs. My many friends, so many beautiful souls, who passed during the HIV crisis. I was so lucky to know you for such a brief time. Professor Leslie Laskey from Washington University in St. Louis, for teaching me how to be a critical thinker. My city planning mentors, Dean Macris and Norman Murdoch. Last but not least, my fellow Old Gays: I treasure our very special, unique relationship.

Mick would like to personally thank: Bill and Jessay for their professionalism, talent, and friendship. Bob, you saved my life. I cherish our friendship. My sister, Carolyn, who's known me the longest, and my extended blood family for their companionship and friendship all these years. Sharilyn, Neil and Peter, and Fred and Jason. My ex Joel Kimmel, for what he has taught me about life, how to be a good person, and for all of the adventures, good and bad. And, of course, our children, Roxy, Ms. Hannah, and Rocky.

The Old Gays always save the best for last: To our followers around the world, thank you thank you thank you. You have changed our lives. You have no idea how much you mean to us. We see you and hear you. Your positive, uplifting comments not only make our day but you're also the reason The Old Gays keep going, aka move gayly forward, every day. You are our inspiration.